# HOLY SPIRIT

# MY

# PRAYER

# PARTNER

"Holy Spirit is Your Divine Prayer Partner, Someone Who Knows the Mind of God Intimately and Can Guide Your Prayers in Alignment with His Will."

TIMOTHY ATUNNISE

Glovim Publishing House
Atlanta, Georgia

# HOLY SPIRIT MY PRAYER PARTNER

Copyright © 2023 by Timothy Atunnise

All rights reserved. No part of this book may be reproduced, copied, stored or transmitted in any form or by any means – graphic, electronic, or mechanical, including photocopying, recording, or information storage and retrieval systems without the prior written permission of Glovim Publishing house except where permitted by law.

Unless otherwise specified, all Scripture quotations in this book are from The Holy Bible, King James Version. KJV is Public domain in the United States printed in 1987.

Glovim Publishing House
1078 Citizens Pkwy
Suite A
Morrow, Georgia 30260

glovimbooks@gmail.com
www.glovimonline.org

Printed in the United States of America

# Table of Contents

Introduction ........................................................................ 7
Holy Spirit as a prayer partner ........................................... 10
The power of prayer and the Holy Spirit............................ 14
Cultivating a relationship with the Holy Spirit .................. 17
Holy Spirit's role in prayer ................................................. 20
Praying in the Spirit............................................................. 24
The fruit of the Spirit and effective prayer......................... 27
Surrendering to the guidance of the Holy Spirit ................ 30
Overcoming obstacles in prayer.......................................... 33
Praying with confidence in the Holy Spirit........................ 37
Partnering with the Holy Spirit for intercession................. 41
The Holy Spirit and the Lord's Prayer................................ 45
Praying in tongues and the Holy Spirit .............................. 48
Discerning the voice of the Holy Spirit in prayer .............. 52
The Holy Spirit's role in spiritual warfare.......................... 56
Walking in the Spirit and effective prayer ......................... 60
Praying for others with the Holy Spirit's help.................... 64
The Holy Spirit and the gift of wisdom in prayer .............. 68
Cultivating a heart of gratitude in prayer ........................... 73
Hearing god'svoice through the Holy Spirit....................... 77
Praying for healing with the Holy Spirit's anointing.......... 80
The Holy Spirit and praying for God's will........................ 84
The Holy Spirit's comfort in times of sorrow..................... 88
Praying with the fruit of Patience and the Holy Spirit ........ 91
The Holy Spirit's Role in Strengthening Your Faith........... 94
Praying for Guidance and Direction....................................98
The Holy Spirit's Role in Answered Prayer ..................... 101
Partnering with the Holy Spirit for Spiritual Growth........ 105
Praying for Revival with the Holy Spirit's fire.................. 109

The Holy Spirit's presence in times of worship ................ 113
Walking in prayerful partnership with the Holy Spirit ..... 116
Other bestselling books from the author .......................... 120

## Introduction

In the depths of the human heart, there exists a profound yearning—a longing that transcends the boundaries of time and space. It is a yearning for a connection, a yearning to commune with the Divine, to find solace in the midst of life's storms, and to draw strength from a source beyond our own frailty. This yearning, dear reader, is a universal call to prayer.

Prayer, often described as the lifeline of faith, is the bridge that connects humanity to the divine realm. It is an age-old practice, woven into the fabric of every major religious tradition, and for the Christian, it is an essential component of their journey with God. Yet, as we embark on this exploration of prayer, we recognize that it is not a solitary endeavor; rather, it is a partnership—an intimate, sacred partnership—with the Holy Spirit.

The title of this book, "Holy Spirit, My Prayer Partner," invites us into the heart of this partnership. It beckons us to delve (as it were) into the depths of a relationship that has often been overshadowed or misunderstood. In the coming pages, we will embark on a journey together—a journey that seeks to unveil the profound role of the Holy Spirit in our prayer lives.

Christianity, at its core, is a faith rooted in relationship—with God, with Jesus Christ, and with one another. Yet, it is in the relationship with the Holy Spirit that we often find ourselves at a crossroads of understanding. Who is the Holy Spirit, and what is His role in our lives?

These questions are foundational, for they lead us to the heart of our partnership in prayer.

The Holy Spirit, often depicted as the third person of the Holy Trinity, is the promised Comforter, the Advocate sent by Jesus Christ Himself. In the words of our Lord, as recorded in the Gospel of John, "And I will ask the Father, and He will give you another Helper, to be with you forever, even the Spirit of truth" (John 14:16-17 ESV). This Helper, the Holy Spirit, is not a distant, ethereal presence; rather, He is a personal, active, and intimate participant in the life of every believer.

As we dig into this partnership with the Holy Spirit, we will uncover the multifaceted nature of His ministry. He is the Comforter who consoles us in our times of grief and distress. He is the Teacher who imparts wisdom and understanding. He is the Empowerer who equips us for service and ministry. And, most importantly, He is the Prayer Partner who intercedes on our behalf with groanings too deep for words (Romans 8:26 ESV).

Throughout the pages of this book, we will explore the transformative power of prayer in partnership with the Holy Spirit. We will journey through the corridors of Scripture, drawing inspiration from the prayers of saints of old who understood the significance of this divine partnership. We will examine the fruits of the Spirit and how they manifest in our prayer lives. We will learn to discern the voice of the Holy Spirit and to walk in step with His guidance. And, above all, we will seek to cultivate a vibrant, life-giving prayer life that is deeply rooted in this partnership.

In the coming chapters, we will encounter stories of believers who have experienced the tangible presence of the Holy Spirit in their prayer closets. We will witness the miraculous, the transformative, and the deeply personal encounters that prayer in partnership with the Holy

Spirit can bring. It is our hope that these narratives will serve as signposts along the way, guiding us toward a deeper, richer, and more authentic prayer experience.

Dear reader, as we embark on this journey together, let us open our hearts and minds to the transformative power of prayer in partnership with the Holy Spirit. Let us cast aside preconceived notions and embrace the profound reality of communion with the Divine. Let us dig into the sacred depths of this partnership, for in doing so, we will find our souls awakened, our faith strengthened, and our lives forever changed.

# Chapter 1

# Holy Spirit as a Prayer Partner

In the quiet moments of our lives, when we bow our heads and close our eyes in prayer, we often do so with a deep longing for a connection with the divine. As Christians, we believe in the power of prayer as a means of communicating with God, seeking His guidance, and finding comfort in times of need. But have you ever considered the Holy Spirit as your prayer partner, the divine companion who walks with you on this sacred journey? In this chapter, we will delve into the profound and extraordinary concept of the Holy Spirit as your prayer partner.

The Divine Presence Within

To truly understand the Holy Spirit's role as a prayer partner, we must first recognize the divine presence within us. In Christian theology, the Holy Spirit is often described as the third person of the Trinity, co-equal with God the Father and God the Son (Jesus Christ). The Holy Spirit is not an abstract concept but a living, dynamic, and personal presence within the heart of every believer.

Imagine, for a moment, that you have a trusted friend who is always by your side, ready to listen to your thoughts, concerns, and desires. This friend knows you intimately, understanding your deepest hopes and fears. The Holy Spirit, as your divine prayer partner, fulfills this role in a way that no earthly friend ever could.

The Gift of Pentecost

The concept of the Holy Spirit as a prayer partner is deeply rooted in the biblical narrative. In the book of Acts, we find the account of Pentecost, a momentous event in the history of Christianity. On that day, as the disciples gathered in one place, a sound like a rushing wind filled the room, and they were filled with the Holy Spirit. Tongues of fire appeared above their heads, and they began to speak in languages they had never learned.

This remarkable event signified the empowerment of the early church through the Holy Spirit. It was a moment when the disciples' understanding of prayer and partnership with the divine was forever transformed. The Holy Spirit was no longer an abstract theological concept; it became a tangible, indwelling presence in their lives.

Praying in the Spirit

One of the most distinctive aspects of partnering with the Holy Spirit in prayer is the practice of praying in the Spirit. This involves speaking in tongues, a spiritual language given by the Holy Spirit. It's a language that transcends human understanding, allowing us to communicate directly with God.

Praying in tongues is a profound experience, often accompanied by a deep sense of peace and spiritual connection. It's a way of bypassing the limitations of our human language and letting the Holy Spirit intercede on our behalf. The Apostle Paul writes about this in Romans 8:26-27, "Likewise, the Spirit helps us in our weakness. For we do not know what to pray for as we ought, but the Spirit himself intercedes for us with groanings too deep for words."

Guidance and Discernment

Another extraordinary aspect of having the Holy Spirit as a prayer partner is the guidance and discernment it offers. The Holy Spirit is not only a listener but also a revealer of God's will. When we seek God's guidance in prayer, the Holy Spirit can provide insight, wisdom, and clarity.

Imagine you are facing a significant decision in your life, one that could have far-reaching consequences. You turn to prayer, seeking God's guidance, and invite the Holy Spirit to lead you. Through a series of impressions, thoughts, and a deep inner knowing, the Holy Spirit guides you toward the right path. This guidance is not mere coincidence or wishful thinking but a tangible manifestation of the Holy Spirit's presence in your life.

The Empowerment of Intercession

Intercessory prayer, the act of praying on behalf of others, is another area where the Holy Spirit excels as a prayer partner. When you lift up the needs, concerns, and struggles of others in prayer, the Holy Spirit partners with you in a powerful way. It's as if you are standing in the gap between heaven and earth, representing the needs of those who cannot pray for themselves.

The Apostle Paul encourages believers to engage in intercessory prayer, saying, "And pray in the Spirit on all occasions with all kinds of prayers and requests. With this in mind, be alert and always keep on praying for all the Lord's people" (Ephesians 6:18, NIV). When you pray in the Spirit for others, you tap into a wellspring of divine compassion and love, and your prayers become instruments of God's grace and healing.

The Transformative Power of Fellowship with the Holy Spirit

As you embark on this journey of partnership with the Holy Spirit in prayer, you'll begin to experience a transformation within yourself. Your prayer life will no longer be a one-sided conversation with the heavens; it will be a dynamic exchange with a loving, attentive, and empowering divine presence.

This partnership will not only impact your prayer life but also your entire walk of faith. You'll find that you are more attuned to the leading of the Holy Spirit in all aspects of your life. You'll experience a deepening of your relationship with God and a greater sense of purpose in your spiritual journey.

The Holy Spirit as your prayer partner is not a theological concept to be understood from a distance; it is a living reality to be experienced in the depths of your soul. This partnership offers a profound and out-of-the-ordinary dimension to your Christian faith. As you continue reading this book, you will explore practical ways to cultivate this partnership, delve into the mysteries of praying in the Spirit, and discover the transformative power of fellowship with the Holy Spirit in your prayer life. Get ready for an extraordinary journey of faith and intimacy with your divine prayer partner, the Holy Spirit.

## Chapter 2

# The Power of Prayer and the Holy Spirit

In the realm of Christian spirituality, prayer is not merely a ritualistic conversation with a distant deity; it is a dynamic connection to the divine, a conduit through which the believer can tap into the boundless power of the Holy Spirit. This chapter delves into the profound and often underappreciated relationship between prayer and the Holy Spirit, unveiling the extraordinary potential that lies within this divine partnership.

The Divine Conversation

Prayer, at its core, is a conversation with God. It's not a one-sided monologue but a dialogue that transcends the confines of time and space. Imagine for a moment that you have been granted an audience with the King of Kings. You stand in the throne room of heaven, and the Creator of the universe invites you to speak, to share your heart's desires, and to seek His wisdom. This is the essence of prayer, and it's a privilege that every believer can access through faith.

The Power of the Holy Spirit

Now, imagine that this divine conversation isn't limited to mere words. It's infused with the power of the Holy Spirit. The Holy Spirit, often referred to as the third person of the Holy Trinity, is not an abstract concept but a living, dynamic presence within the believer. When you pray, you invite the Holy Spirit into the conversation, and that changes everything.

## Intercessor and Advocate

The Bible tells us that the Holy Spirit is our intercessor and advocate. In Romans 8:26-27 (NIV), it says, "In the same way, the Spirit helps us in our weakness. We do not know what we ought to pray for, but the Spirit himself intercedes for us through wordless groans. And he who searches our hearts knows the mind of the Spirit because the Spirit intercedes for God's people in accordance with the will of God."

Think about the implications of this. When you don't know how to pray or are too overwhelmed to find the right words, the Holy Spirit steps in. He understands the deepest desires of your heart and aligns your prayers with the will of God. Your prayers become divinely guided missiles aimed at the very heart of God's purposes.

## Access to Heavenly Resources

The power of the Holy Spirit in prayer is not limited to words alone. It extends to accessing heavenly resources. In Acts 1:8 (NIV), Jesus tells His disciples, "But you will receive power when the Holy Spirit comes on you; and you will be my witnesses in Jerusalem, and in all Judea and Samaria, and to the ends of the earth." This power isn't just for witnessing; it's for every aspect of the believer's life, including prayer.

When you pray in the power of the Holy Spirit, you tap into the supernatural resources of heaven. You are no longer bound by your own limitations but are empowered by the limitless might of God. Your prayers become instruments of transformation, not only in your life but in the world around you.

The Extraordinary in the Ordinary

To truly grasp the power of prayer and the Holy Spirit, one must be willing to embrace the extraordinary in the midst of the ordinary. Prayer is not a mundane task to be checked off a list; it is a cosmic adventure in communion with the divine.

Imagine, as you pray, the Holy Spirit moving like a mighty wind, stirring the very atmosphere around you. Picture angels heeding the call of your petitions, carrying out divine assignments on your behalf. Envision breakthroughs, healings, and miracles flowing from your prayers like a river of living water.

A Bold Invitation

This chapter invites you to a bold and audacious journey—a journey into the depths of prayer, where the Holy Spirit is not merely a theological concept but a living, breathing reality. It challenges you to see prayer as an act of partnership with the Divine, where the ordinary becomes extraordinary, and the impossible becomes possible.

As you continue your exploration of this divine partnership, remember that you are not alone in your prayers. The Holy Spirit stands ready to empower, guide, and intercede for you. Embrace the power of prayer and the Holy Spirit, and watch as your faith soars to new heights, and your life becomes a testimony to the limitless grace and love of God.

## Chapter 3

# Cultivating a Relationship with the Holy Spirit

In the realm of Christian faith, there is perhaps no relationship more profound, transformative, and intimate than that which believers share with the Holy Spirit. To embark on this journey of cultivating a relationship with the Holy Spirit is to delve (explore deeply) into the very heart of your faith, where the ordinary becomes extraordinary, the mundane is infused with divine purpose, and the limits of human understanding are transcended.

The Divine Paradox

Before we delve into the practical aspects of cultivating a relationship with the Holy Spirit, let us first address the divine paradox that defines this relationship. The Holy Spirit, often described as the third person of the Trinity, is both transcendent and immanent, omnipotent yet gentle, infinite yet personal. Embracing this paradox is essential as we seek to understand and experience the Holy Spirit's presence in our lives.

The Indwelling Presence

One of the foundational truths of cultivating a relationship with the Holy Spirit is recognizing the indwelling presence of the Spirit within every believer. In Christianity, the moment of salvation is not merely a legal transaction but a profound spiritual transformation. At that instant, the Holy Spirit takes up residence within the believer's heart. This is not a casual visitation but a permanent dwelling. Understanding this truth is the first step in cultivating a relationship with the Holy Spirit.

## The Still, Small Voice

In the bustling noise of our daily lives, it's easy to overlook the gentle whisper of the Holy Spirit. Cultivating a relationship with the Holy Spirit requires us to attune our spiritual ears to the still, small voice. This voice is not always audible but is a deep impression on our hearts and minds. It's the nudge that prompts us to show kindness to a stranger, the prompting to pray for a friend in need, or the wisdom that guides us in making crucial life decisions.

## The Dance of Surrender

To cultivate a relationship with the Holy Spirit is to enter into a dance of surrender. It's a surrender of our will to God's will, a surrender of our desires to His desires. This surrender is not a defeat but a glorious victory, for in surrendering, we open the door for the Holy Spirit to work powerfully in our lives. It's a dance where we yield our plans, ambitions, and fears, and allow the Holy Spirit to lead us into the divine choreography of life.

## The Word and the Spirit

The Bible is often referred to as the written Word of God, but it is through the Holy Spirit that the living Word of God is revealed to us. Cultivating a relationship with the Holy Spirit involves an intimate engagement with Scripture, where the written words come alive with divine revelation. The Holy Spirit illuminates the words of Scripture, unveiling deep spiritual truths, and providing us with guidance, comfort, and conviction.

## The Fruits and Gifts

As our relationship with the Holy Spirit deepens, we begin to bear the fruits of the Spirit - love, joy, peace, patience, kindness, goodness, faithfulness, gentleness, and self-control. These fruits are the outward evidence of an inner transformation brought about by the Holy Spirit. Additionally, the Holy Spirit bestows upon believers spiritual gifts for the edification of the Church and the advancement of God's kingdom.

## The Power and Presence

Cultivating a relationship with the Holy Spirit unleashes a divine power in our lives. It's a power that enables us to overcome sin, heal the brokenhearted, and speak boldly in the name of Jesus. It's a power that empowers us to live a life that is extraordinary, marked by supernatural encounters and divine interventions. It's a power that transforms ordinary believers into vessels of God's extraordinary grace.

## The Fellowship of the Holy Spirit

Ultimately, cultivating a relationship with the Holy Spirit leads us into a deep and abiding fellowship with God Himself. It's an intimacy that goes beyond words, a communion of hearts, and a union of spirits. It's a fellowship that satisfies the deepest longings of our souls and brings us into the very presence of the Almighty.

Cultivating a relationship with the Holy Spirit is a journey that defies the ordinary and embraces the extraordinary. It's a journey of surrender, revelation, transformation, and empowerment. It's a journey that leads us into the heart of God, where the divine paradox of the Holy Spirit becomes a glorious reality in our lives.

# Chapter 4

# The Divine Intercessor: Holy Spirit's Role in Prayer

In the realm of prayer, Christians often find themselves at the intersection of faith and the supernatural. It is here, in this divine rendezvous, that the Holy Spirit emerges as the unsung hero of intercession. This chapter delves deep into the extraordinary role of the Holy Spirit in prayer, unveiling its mystical, transformative, and empowering aspects.

The Paraclete: Our Divine Advocate

Before we embark on this exploration, it's crucial to understand the Holy Spirit's biblical identity as the Paraclete. In John 14:16, Jesus promised to send the Paraclete, which is often translated as the Comforter or Helper. But this word encompasses far more than mere comfort. Paraclete implies an advocate, a legal representative who stands alongside us in our time of need. In the context of prayer, the Holy Spirit becomes our divine lawyer, pleading our case before the heavenly court.

The Language of Heaven

In the Christian tradition, prayer is often described as a conversation with God. But what if I told you that this conversation transcends mere words? The Holy Spirit introduces us to the celestial dialect - the language of heaven itself. In Romans 8:26, we're told that "the Spirit helps us in our weakness. For we do not know what to pray for as we ought, but the Spirit himself intercedes for us with groanings too deep for words."

This is not a mere metaphor. It is a reality. The Holy Spirit, in its infinite wisdom, translates our inarticulate cries into the perfect petitions that align with God's will. When we pray, we might stumble over our words, but the Holy Spirit refines our prayers into divine poetry.

The Holy Spirit's Blueprint for Prayer

Imagine your prayer life as a blueprint for a magnificent cathedral. The Holy Spirit is the master architect. It knows the grand design of God's will and can guide you in constructing the most beautiful and purposeful prayers. It is the Holy Spirit that whispers into your spirit, directing you towards the very heart of God's desires.

When you pray in sync with the Holy Spirit, your prayers cease to be a laundry list of desires and become a symphony of alignment with the divine will. This alignment brings about a profound sense of purpose and fulfillment, as your prayers become instruments in the orchestra of God's master plan.

Accessing the Heavenly Control Room

In the realm of prayer, the Holy Spirit grants you access to the heavenly control room. You become a co-laborer with God, partnering in the creation of miracles and transformation. When you pray, it's not merely sending your requests to the heavens and hoping for a response; it's engaging in a supernatural collaboration with the Creator Himself.

Think of prayer as a cosmic conference call, with the Holy Spirit as your spiritual satellite connection. As you pray, the Holy Spirit translates your petitions into heavenly frequencies, causing spiritual shifts, angelic movements, and divine interventions.

Praying in the Spirit

To fully grasp the Holy Spirit's role in prayer, we must explore the concept of praying in the Spirit. This practice involves uttering words and sounds beyond our natural understanding - often referred to as praying in tongues. It is a unique form of communication between your spirit and God's Spirit.

Praying in the Spirit bypasses the limitations of human language and intellect. It's like plugging into a direct spiritual hotline, where the Holy Spirit takes the lead, expressing the deepest desires and needs of your soul. It's a powerful way to pray when you're uncertain about what to pray for, as it allows the Spirit to intercede on your behalf with perfect clarity.

The Supernatural Alignment

Picture a ship guided by a skilled captain through treacherous waters. The Holy Spirit serves as your celestial navigator, ensuring that your prayers stay on course. It aligns your petitions with God's character, promises, and purposes.

This supernatural alignment is the secret to effective prayer. When your desires align with God's desires, there's an irresistible force at play. It's akin to a river merging with the ocean - the river's flow is absorbed and transformed by the vastness of the sea. Your prayers, aligned with God's will through the Holy Spirit, become a force of divine impact in the world.

Embracing the Divine Partnership

The Holy Spirit's role in prayer transcends the ordinary and ventures into the extraordinary. It is a divine partnership that empowers, transforms, and transcends human limitations. Through the Holy Spirit, prayer becomes a supernatural conversation, a blueprint for God's will, and a journey into the heavenly control room. It is an invitation to pray in the Spirit, align with God's purposes, and embrace the extraordinary power of divine intercession.

As we continue our journey in this book, remember that the Holy Spirit is not a passive observer in your prayer life. It is your divine advocate, the one who translates your heart's cries into heaven's language. Embrace this partnership, and you will discover that in prayer, you are never alone. You are joined by the infinite wisdom and power of the Holy Spirit, making your prayers bold, extraordinary, and truly out of the ordinary.

## Chapter 5

# Praying in the Spirit: What it Means

In the realm of Christian spirituality, few concepts are as enigmatic and yet profoundly transformative as "praying in the Spirit." This chapter aims to unravel the mysteries behind this practice and shed light on its significance from a Christian perspective, taking you on a journey that goes beyond the ordinary.

The Essence of Praying in the Spirit

At its core, praying in the Spirit is an intimate and mysterious connection between the believer and the divine. It's a form of prayer that transcends mere words and taps into the depths of the soul. In 1 Corinthians 14:14-15, the Apostle Paul writes, "For if I pray in a tongue, my spirit prays, but my mind is unfruitful. What am I to do? I will pray with my spirit, but I will pray with my mind also; I will sing praise with my spirit, but I will sing with my mind also."

This passage hints at the dual nature of praying in the Spirit. It engages the spirit, which goes beyond the limitations of the intellect and taps into the supernatural. This form of prayer is marked by a sense of surrender, where the believer yields to the Holy Spirit, allowing Him to pray through them.

The Language of the Spirit: Glossolalia

One aspect of praying in the Spirit is the phenomenon known as glossolalia or speaking in tongues. This is the use of an unknown language during prayer, a language given by the Holy Spirit. It's not a human language but rather a heavenly one. Speaking in tongues is like a divine code, a secret language between the believer and God.

When one prays in tongues, they bypass their own understanding, allowing the Holy Spirit to intercede on their behalf. Romans 8:26-27 elucidates this beautifully: "Likewise, the Spirit helps us in our weakness. For we do not know what to pray for as we ought, but the Spirit himself intercedes for us with groanings too deep for words. And he who searches hearts knows what is the mind of the Spirit because the Spirit intercedes for the saints according to the will of God."

Praying in tongues is a bold and out-of-the-ordinary experience. It's an act of complete trust in the Holy Spirit, surrendering the need for control and relying on God's wisdom and guidance in prayer. This practice enables believers to express their deepest emotions, desires, and supplications in a way that transcends human language.

Unlocking the Supernatural

Praying in the Spirit unlocks the supernatural dimensions of prayer. It's a direct line of communication with the Creator, unencumbered by the limitations of the natural world. When we pray in the Spirit, we enter a realm where the Spirit of God becomes our prayer partner in the most intimate sense.

The Apostle Jude, in verse 20 of his epistle, encourages believers to "build yourselves up in your most holy faith and pray in the Holy Spirit." This suggests that praying in the Spirit not only strengthens our faith but also aligns our prayers with God's divine will.

The Out-of-the-Ordinary Results

Praying in the Spirit yields extraordinary results. It brings about a sense of peace and spiritual refreshment. It's a powerful tool in spiritual warfare, as it allows the believer to stand firm against the schemes of the enemy. The Apostle Paul, in Ephesians 6:18, emphasizes the importance of praying in the Spirit as part of the spiritual armor: "praying at all times in the Spirit, with all prayer and supplication."

Moreover, praying in the Spirit often leads to insights, revelations, and discernment. It's as though the believer's spiritual senses are heightened, enabling them to grasp the deeper truths of God's Word and His plans for their life.

An Extraordinary Invitation

Praying in the Spirit is an extraordinary invitation to commune with the divine. It's a practice that defies the ordinary boundaries of human understanding and transcends the limitations of language. It's a bold act of faith and surrender, allowing the Holy Spirit to intercede on our behalf.

To truly grasp the depth of this practice, one must be willing to step out of the ordinary, to embrace the mystery, and to trust in the supernatural work of the Holy Spirit. In doing so, believers can experience a level of intimacy with God that goes beyond words, an intimacy that transforms their prayer life and their entire walk of faith.

## Chapter 6

## The Fruit of the Spirit and Effective Prayer

In the realm of Christian spirituality, the concept of the "Fruit of the Spirit" is often hailed as one of the most profound and transformative aspects of the faith. Rooted in Galatians 5:22-23, it reads: "But the fruit of the Spirit is love, joy, peace, forbearance, kindness, goodness, faithfulness, gentleness and self-control. Against such things there is no law." These nine attributes encapsulate the transformative power of the Holy Spirit in the life of a believer, and they also play a pivotal role in shaping the landscape of effective prayer.

Let's delve (pun unintended) into how each aspect of the Fruit of the Spirit can enhance and deepen your prayer life, providing a unique perspective on this essential topic.

1. Love: The Foundation of Prayer

Love, as the foremost fruit of the Spirit, serves as the foundation of effective prayer. When we approach God with a heart filled with love, our prayers become an outpouring of genuine affection and devotion. Love bridges the gap between the finite and the infinite, allowing us to connect with the Creator on an intimate level. In prayer, we express our love for God, our neighbors, and even our enemies, aligning our desires with His perfect will.

2. Joy: The Strength in Prayer

Prayer is not merely a solemn duty but a source of immeasurable joy. The joy of the Lord becomes our strength (Nehemiah 8:10), and it infuses our prayers with enthusiasm and confidence. In times of trial, joy sustains us, enabling us to pray with resilience and unwavering trust in God's goodness.

3. Peace: The Calm Amidst the Storm

In the chaos of life, the fruit of peace provides a tranquil sanctuary in our prayers. It allows us to approach God with a composed spirit, even in the face of adversity. Peace grants us the assurance that God is in control, calming our anxieties and fostering an atmosphere of serenity in our prayer closet.

4. Forbearance: Patience in Prayer

Forbearance, often translated as patience, is a virtue indispensable in prayer. Effective prayer requires persistence, and forbearance helps us persevere in seeking God's face. It teaches us to trust God's timing, even when our prayers seem unanswered, knowing that His plans are always for our good.

5. Kindness and Goodness: Compassion in Intercession

Intercessory prayer, where we stand in the gap for others, is an act of kindness and goodness. These fruits of the Spirit empower us to pray with genuine compassion, lifting up the needs and concerns of those around us. Our prayers become a channel through which God's kindness and goodness flow into the lives of others.

6. Faithfulness: Consistency in Communication

Effective prayer requires consistency. The fruit of faithfulness encourages us to maintain a steadfast prayer life, not wavering in our devotion to God. Just as God is faithful to His promises, we are called to be faithful in our communication with Him.

7. Gentleness: Humility in Petition

When we approach God in prayer, gentleness is key. It reminds us of our humble position before the Almighty. A gentle spirit in prayer acknowledges our dependence on God's mercy and grace, fostering a spirit of humility that is pleasing to Him.

8. Self-Control: Discipline in Devotion

Self-control is vital in maintaining a disciplined prayer life. It helps us resist distractions and prioritize our time with God. By exercising self-control, we can dedicate ourselves to fervent and focused prayer, deepening our connection with the divine.

The Fruit of the Spirit is not just a beautiful list of qualities; it is a roadmap to a rich and vibrant prayer life. As we cultivate these virtues through the guidance of the Holy Spirit, our prayers become more than words; they become a profound communion with the living God. So, let your prayers be infused with love, joy, peace, forbearance, kindness, goodness, faithfulness, gentleness, and self-control, and watch as your relationship with God blossoms into a transformative journey of faith.

## Chapter 7

## Surrendering to the Guidance of the Holy Spirit

In the journey of faith, surrender is a concept of paramount importance. It is the act of yielding ourselves to a higher power, acknowledging our own limitations, and allowing divine guidance to lead us. In this chapter, we delve deep into the profound experience of surrendering to the guidance of the Holy Spirit from a Christian perspective.

The Nature of Surrender

Surrendering to the guidance of the Holy Spirit begins with understanding the nature of this divine relationship. It's not merely submitting to a set of rules or rituals but engaging in an intimate, dynamic partnership with the third person of the Holy Trinity. This partnership is characterized by love, trust, and communion.

To surrender to the Holy Spirit means letting go of our self-reliance and ego-driven desires. It means recognizing that our finite wisdom and understanding cannot compare to the infinite knowledge and wisdom of God. Surrender is the act of laying down our pride, control, and preconceived notions at the feet of the Divine.

The Dance of Surrender

Imagine a dance where you are led by a skilled partner. In this dance, you are not in control; you trust your partner's lead. Surrendering to the Holy Spirit is like this dance. The Holy Spirit is the master choreographer of our lives, leading us with grace and precision through the intricate steps of God's divine plan.

This surrender is not passive; it's a joyful participation. It's allowing the Holy Spirit to take the lead, guiding our steps, and orchestrating the music of our lives. It's an exhilarating and liberating experience where we move in harmony with the Spirit's promptings, no longer stumbling in darkness but walking in the light of God's wisdom.

The Trust Factor

Surrender also requires an immense amount of trust. We must trust that the Holy Spirit has our best interests at heart, that His guidance is always for our ultimate good. This trust is built on the foundation of our faith in God's character, His love, and His promises.

It's acknowledging that God's plan is far grander and more beautiful than anything we could envision. Surrendering to the guidance of the Holy Spirit is an act of acknowledging our limitations and God's unlimited potential. It's trusting that even in the most challenging moments of life, the Holy Spirit is there, working all things together for our good (Romans 8:28).

The Surrendered Mind

One of the most transformative aspects of surrendering to the Holy Spirit is the renewal of the mind. As we relinquish control and submit to God's guidance, our thought patterns and perspectives change. Our focus shifts from worldly concerns to heavenly priorities.

The surrendered mind is filled with peace, for it knows that God is in control. It is free from anxiety, doubt, and fear, because it relies on the steadfast love of the Spirit. Surrendering the mind to the Holy Spirit allows us to see the world through God's eyes, to discern His will in all circumstances, and to make choices that align with His purposes.

## The Power of Surrendered Prayer

Prayer is the vehicle through which we communicate with the Holy Spirit. Surrendered prayer is not a wish list presented to God; it's a sacred conversation with the Divine. It's an opportunity to pour out our hearts, listen to the Spirit's gentle whispers, and receive divine guidance.

When we surrender in prayer, we open ourselves to the supernatural. Miracles happen, chains are broken, and the impossible becomes possible. Surrendered prayer is a dialogue where we align our desires with God's will and allow the Holy Spirit to intercede on our behalf, translating our imperfect words into perfect petitions before the throne of grace (Romans 8:26-27).

## A Life Transformed by Surrender

Surrendering to the guidance of the Holy Spirit is not a one-time event but a lifelong journey. It's a path marked by growth, transformation, and deepening intimacy with God. As we surrender, we experience the freedom that comes from trusting in God's sovereignty. We find purpose and fulfillment in aligning our will with His, and we witness the extraordinary work of the Spirit in our lives.

In the grand tapestry of faith, surrender is the thread that weaves our story into God's story. It is the bold and out-of-the-ordinary decision to yield ourselves to the Divine Choreographer, trusting that His guidance will lead us into a life of extraordinary purpose and eternal significance. Surrender, then, is not weakness; it is the ultimate act of faith and courage.

## Chapter 8

## Overcoming Obstacles in Prayer with the Holy Spirit

In the journey of faith, prayer stands as one of the most potent and intimate channels of communication between the believer and their Creator. It is a direct line to the heart of God, a sacred dialogue where our deepest longings, hopes, and fears are laid bare before the throne of grace. But as profound as prayer is, it is not without its challenges and obstacles that can leave us feeling disconnected and disheartened. In this chapter, we delve into the transformative power of the Holy Spirit in overcoming these obstacles, drawing from the depths of Christian spirituality to guide us.

The Silent Struggle

One of the most profound obstacles in prayer is the silence that often meets our petitions. We've all been there, haven't we? Those moments when our cries seem to echo in an empty room, and the heavens remain seemingly unresponsive. It's in these moments that doubt and discouragement can creep in, causing us to question the effectiveness of our prayers.

But let us consider this: the silence of God in prayer is not a sign of His absence or indifference. It's an invitation to dive deeper into the wellspring of faith. The Holy Spirit, our ever-present prayer partner, is there to guide us through this silent struggle. He invites us to pray with perseverance, reminding us of the parable of the persistent widow (Luke 18:1-8). Through the power of the Holy Spirit, we can find the strength to keep knocking on heaven's door, knowing that God hears and responds in His perfect timing.

The Battle of Distractions

In a world filled with constant noise and distraction, finding the focus to engage in meaningful prayer can be a Herculean task. The allure of technology, the demands of our daily lives, and the ever-increasing pace of the world can pull us away from the sacred space of prayer. But this is where the Holy Spirit shines as our prayer partner.

The Holy Spirit is our divine filter, helping us sift through the noise and chaos of life to find that quiet inner chamber where we can commune with God. In those moments of stillness, the Spirit gently whispers, guiding our thoughts and aligning our hearts with the will of the Father. Through the Holy Spirit, we learn to embrace the discipline of solitude and silence, finding that in the midst of life's cacophony, the voice of God can be heard with crystal clarity.

The Weight of Unforgiveness

Unforgiveness can be a heavy burden to bear, and it acts as a formidable roadblock in our prayer life. When we harbor bitterness and resentment, it's like a dark cloud that obscures our vision of God's grace. But the Holy Spirit is the gentle wind that blows away this cloud, revealing the radiant face of God's love.

As our prayer partner, the Holy Spirit teaches us the transformative power of forgiveness. He reminds us of Christ's words in Matthew 6:14-15, "For if you forgive others their trespasses, your heavenly Father will also forgive you, but if you do not forgive others their trespasses, neither will your Father forgive your trespasses." Through His guidance, we find the strength to release the chains of unforgiveness, allowing our prayers to flow freely, unencumbered by bitterness.

The Thorn of Doubt

Doubt can be a relentless thorn in the side of our faith, and it often rears its head when we approach God in prayer. We wonder, "Does God really hear me? Does He care about my needs?" These doubts can erode our confidence and hinder the fullness of our prayer life.

Yet, the Holy Spirit is the oil of faith that soothes the irritation of doubt. He reminds us that faith is not the absence of doubt but the courage to pray in spite of it. He directs our gaze to Hebrews 11:6, which says, "And without faith, it is impossible to please him, for whoever would draw near to God must believe that he exists and that he rewards those who seek him." Through the Holy Spirit's guidance, we learn to anchor our prayers in faith, trusting that our Heavenly Father is indeed attentive to our cries.

The Valley of Desolation

There are seasons in life when we find ourselves in the valley of desolation, where circumstances seem hopeless, and our prayers feel like feeble whispers in the wind. In these moments of despair, it's easy to lose heart and abandon our prayer life altogether.

Yet, the Holy Spirit is our unwavering companion in the valley. He reminds us of Psalm 23:4, "Even though I walk through the valley of the shadow of death, I will fear no evil, for you are with me; your rod and your staff, they comfort me." With the Holy Spirit as our guide, we discover that even in the darkest moments, our prayers are not in vain. They become like seeds sown in the fertile soil of God's providence, waiting for the appointed time of harvest.

The Prayerful Partnership

The Holy Spirit is not merely a passive observer of our prayers; He is an active participant, our prayer partner. He empowers us to overcome the obstacles that can hinder our communication with God. Through His guidance, we learn to persist in prayer, find focus in the midst of distractions, release the burden of unforgiveness, conquer doubt with faith, and trust in the darkest valleys.

As we cultivate our relationship with the Holy Spirit, our prayer life transforms from a routine to a profound journey of intimacy with the Creator. With the Holy Spirit as our prayer partner, we discover that prayer is not just a religious duty but a dynamic and life-changing conversation with the One who knows us intimately and loves us unconditionally. In this partnership, we find the strength to overcome every obstacle and draw nearer to the heart of God.

## Chapter 9

## Praying with Confidence in the Holy Spirit

In the journey of faith, prayer stands as a bridge that connects our human hearts with the divine. It is the lifeline through which we communicate with our Creator, seeking guidance, solace, and power. Yet, for many, prayer can be shrouded in doubt and uncertainty. We often wonder if our words reach beyond the ceiling, if God hears our pleas, and if our requests align with His divine will. In this chapter, we will explore the profound transformation that occurs when we learn to pray with unwavering confidence in the Holy Spirit. It's a journey that takes us beyond the ordinary and into the extraordinary realms of faith.

The Foundation of Confidence

To pray with confidence in the Holy Spirit, we must first understand the foundation upon which this confidence is built. It is rooted in an unshakable trust in God's character and promises. The Bible assures us that God is faithful, unchanging, and all-powerful. He is the same yesterday, today, and forever. Therefore, when we approach Him in prayer, we can do so with absolute confidence that He is listening, and He cares for us.

"Let us then approach God's throne of grace with confidence, so that we may receive mercy and find grace to help us in our time of need." (Hebrews 4:16, NIV)

The Role of the Holy Spirit

Central to our confidence in prayer is the understanding of the Holy Spirit's role as our Helper and Intercessor. When we invite the Holy Spirit into our prayer life, we tap into a supernatural source of wisdom, guidance, and power. The Holy Spirit not only assists us in articulating our needs but also aligns our prayers with God's perfect will.

"In the same way, the Spirit helps us in our weakness. We do not know what we ought to pray for, but the Spirit himself intercedes for us through wordless groans." (Romans 8:26, NIV)

Imagine the Holy Spirit as a skilled translator who takes our imperfect, human words and presents them before God in a language that transcends human limitations. It is through this divine partnership that our prayers become bold and effective.

Confidence in Identity

To pray with unwavering confidence in the Holy Spirit, we must also recognize our identity as children of God. We are not strangers or beggars approaching a distant deity, but rather, we are beloved sons and daughters of the King. This understanding transforms our posture in prayer.

When we pray with confidence in our identity, we approach God as a child approaches a loving parent. We come with the assurance that our Heavenly Father desires to bless us, guide us, and meet our needs. This confidence is not rooted in our own worthiness but in the finished work of Christ on the cross, which has made us righteous before God.

"See what great love the Father has lavished on us, that we should be called children of God!" (1 John 3:1, NIV)

Experiencing the Extraordinary

As we cultivate confidence in the Holy Spirit, we begin to experience the extraordinary in our prayer life. Miracles, signs, and wonders become more than just historical accounts; they become the present reality of our faith journey. Boldness replaces doubt, and we see prayers answered in ways that exceed our expectations.

"Now to him who is able to do immeasurably more than all we ask or imagine, according to his power that is at work within us..." (Ephesians 3:20, NIV)

The Holy Spirit empowers us to pray audacious prayers, to believe for the impossible, and to witness the supernatural unfold before our eyes. We become partakers in the divine mysteries, co-laborers with God in His grand plan for redemption.

Practical Steps

Praying with confidence in the Holy Spirit requires both faith and practice. Here are some practical steps to help you embark on this extraordinary journey:

1. Cultivate Intimacy: Spend time in worship, reading the Word, and communing with God. The more intimately you know Him, the more confident you'll be in approaching Him.

2. Listen to the Spirit: Pay attention to the gentle whispers, promptings, and convictions of the Holy Spirit. He will guide your prayers and reveal God's will.

3. Declare God's Promises: Speak God's promises and truths over your life. The Word of God is a powerful weapon that bolsters your confidence.

4. Boldly Ask: Don't be afraid to ask for what you need. Be specific in your prayers and trust that God hears and answers according to His will.

5. Expect the Extraordinary: Anticipate that God will move in remarkable ways. Keep your eyes open for answered prayers and divine interventions.

Praying with confidence in the Holy Spirit is not a mere religious ritual; it's a supernatural adventure that leads us into deeper intimacy with God. As we shed doubt and embrace unwavering trust, our prayers transcend the ordinary and usher us into the extraordinary. In this partnership with the Holy Spirit, we discover that the impossible is possible, and our faith soars to new heights. So, go ahead, step out of the ordinary, and embark on this extraordinary journey of confident prayer in the power of the Holy Spirit.

## Chapter 10

## Partnering with the Holy Spirit for Intercession

In the realm of prayer, intercession stands as a potent spiritual force, a divine partnership between humanity and the Holy Spirit that transcends the ordinary bounds of communication. It is a sacred bridge connecting our earthly existence with the heavenly realm, where our petitions and supplications are brought before the throne of God. In this chapter, we will delve deeply into the profound art of intercession and explore how, from a Christian perspective, we can partner with the Holy Spirit in this extraordinary practice.

The Divine Invitation to Intercede

Intercession is a divine invitation extended to believers, a call to step into the role of spiritual ambassadors, representing both the needs of humanity and the heart of God. In the Bible, we find countless examples of intercessors who stood in the gap between God and humanity. Abraham interceded for the city of Sodom, Moses for the rebellious Israelites, and Jesus himself interceded for his disciples and all believers. We are beckoned to follow in their footsteps, taking up the mantle of intercessory prayer.

The Holy Spirit: Our Intercessor and Partner

Before we delve deeper into our role as intercessors, we must recognize the essential partner in this divine endeavor—the Holy Spirit. In Romans 8:26, we are reminded that "the Spirit helps us in our weakness.

We do not know what we ought to pray for, but the Spirit himself intercedes for us through wordless groans." This verse unveils the profound truth that the Holy Spirit is not only our Helper but our divine Intercessor.

The Holy Spirit possesses an intimate knowledge of our hearts, needs, and desires. He transcends language and communicates with God on our behalf in ways that go beyond our understanding. When we yield ourselves to the Spirit's leading, we become conduits through which His intercession flows.

The Art of Spirit-Led Intercession

Effective intercession involves yielding our will and desires to the Holy Spirit's guidance. It's a partnership marked by sensitivity to His promptings and a willingness to be vessels through which His intercessory work can manifest. Here are some key principles to consider:

1. Alignment with God's Will: Intercessory prayer isn't about imposing our desires on God but aligning our hearts with His divine will. The Holy Spirit helps us discern God's purposes and desires in specific situations.

2. Deep Empathy: Intercession requires a profound empathy for the needs and struggles of others. As we partner with the Holy Spirit, He imparts His compassion to us, enabling us to pray with genuine concern.

3. Persistent Prayer: Jesus encouraged persistent prayer, and intercession often involves continued, fervent supplication. The Holy Spirit provides the stamina and endurance needed for prolonged intercession.

4. Spiritual Warfare: Intercession is not limited to requesting blessings but also involves engaging in spiritual warfare. The Holy Spirit equips us with spiritual weapons to combat the forces of darkness.

5. Prophetic Intercession: In some instances, the Holy Spirit may lead us into prophetic intercession, where we pray with insight into future events or situations. This requires a deep trust in His guidance.

The Holy Spirit's Groans and Wordless Intercession

One of the most mysterious aspects of partnering with the Holy Spirit in intercession is His wordless groans. Romans 8:26 speaks of this phenomenon, highlighting that when we don't know what to pray, the Spirit intercedes with groans that words cannot express.

These wordless intercessions are a profound expression of the Holy Spirit's intimate connection with our innermost beings. They transcend language barriers and reach the depths of our souls, conveying our deepest longings and needs to God. When we allow ourselves to be carried by these groans, we enter a realm of intercession that transcends the limitations of human speech.

The Impact of Spirit-Led Intercession

The impact of intercession, when led by the Holy Spirit, cannot be overstated. Lives are transformed, nations are changed, and the very course of history can be altered through the prayers of intercessors. As we partner with the Spirit in this divine endeavor, we become instruments of God's grace and vessels of His power.

Let us embrace the extraordinary privilege of partnering with the Holy Spirit for intercession. It is a divine invitation to participate in God's redemptive work on Earth, a sacred journey where our prayers intersect with the heavenly realm. As we yield to the Holy Spirit's leading, we tap into a wellspring of spiritual power and experience the awe-inspiring reality of being co-laborers with God in the realm of intercession.

## Chapter 11

## The Holy Spirit and the Lord's Prayer

In this chapter, we embark on a profound journey into the heart of Christian spirituality, exploring the sacred bond between the Holy Spirit and the Lord's Prayer. Prepare to delve into the extraordinary realm where divine guidance and human supplication converge.

The Unveiling of the Lord's Prayer

The Lord's Prayer, also known as the "Our Father," stands as a cornerstone of Christian devotion, a gift from Jesus Himself to His disciples. Yet, few realize the profound connection it shares with the Holy Spirit.

Picture this: Jesus, the Son of God, stood among His disciples, teaching them how to pray. As He uttered those sacred words, "Our Father who art in heaven," the very breath that carried these words bore the essence of the Holy Spirit. In that moment, the divine connection between the Father, the Son, and the Spirit was unveiled.

The Invocation of the Triune God

In the Lord's Prayer, we invoke the name of the Father, recognizing Him as our heavenly Parent, the source of all wisdom and providence. We acknowledge His holiness and sovereignty, aligning our will with His divine plan. But it doesn't stop there.

The Holy Spirit, the often-overlooked member of the Holy Trinity, stands beside us as we utter those words. As we say, "Thy will be done on earth as it is in heaven," we invite the Spirit to infuse our hearts and minds with divine wisdom, guidance, and understanding. In essence, we are invoking the Triune God - Father, Son, and Holy Spirit - to be actively present in our prayers.

The Power of Alignment

Consider this: The Lord's Prayer begins with a focus on God's name, kingdom, and will, not our own needs. This order is not arbitrary but profoundly significant. It teaches us the power of aligning our desires with God's divine purpose.

The Holy Spirit, the divine Advocate, plays a pivotal role in this alignment process. When we surrender our will to God's, the Spirit empowers us to pray with a pure heart, free from selfish motives. Through His transformative work, our desires are shaped in conformity to God's will, making our petitions resonate with heaven itself.

The Forgiveness Imperative

"As we forgive those who trespass against us" - these words from the Lord's Prayer hold a staggering truth. Forgiveness is not merely a suggestion but an imperative. It is the cornerstone of our relationship with God and others.

The Holy Spirit, the Comforter and Convicter, is the divine agent of forgiveness. He convicts us of our need to forgive and empowers us to extend grace to those who have wronged us. As we yield to His leading, our hearts are softened, and the healing power of forgiveness flows through us.

## Lead Us Not Into Temptation

In the final part of the Lord's Prayer, we plead, "Lead us not into temptation, but deliver us from evil." Here, the Holy Spirit is our divine shield, our protector against the forces of darkness. When we pray this line, we are enlisting the Spirit's aid in our spiritual battles.

The Holy Spirit equips us with spiritual discernment, guiding us away from the snares of temptation. He empowers us to stand firm against evil, providing strength and courage in times of trial.

## The Divine Synergy

In the Lord's Prayer, we find a divine symphony of Father, Son, and Holy Spirit working in perfect harmony. It is a prayer that transcends mere words; it is a conduit through which the triune God intersects with our lives.

As Christians, we must not overlook the Holy Spirit's role in this sacred prayer. He is the unseen, yet ever-present guide who empowers us to pray with fervor, purity, and alignment with God's will. When we pray the Lord's Prayer, we do so with the confidence that the Spirit is interceding on our behalf, bridging the gap between earth and heaven.

In the next chapter, we will explore the transformative impact of praying in tongues and the Holy Spirit's profound role in this extraordinary gift of the Spirit. Brace yourself for a journey into the supernatural realm of prayer empowered by the Holy Spirit.

## Chapter 12

## Praying in Tongues and the Holy Spirit

In the realm of Christian spirituality, few topics have sparked as much intrigue, curiosity, and debate as the practice of praying in tongues. This phenomenon, closely associated with the presence and work of the Holy Spirit, has inspired awe and confusion in equal measure. In this chapter, we will delve into the depths of praying in tongues, seeking to demystify and illuminate this unique aspect of Christian prayer. Prepare to journey beyond the ordinary, for we are about to explore a spiritual landscape that is at once ancient and mysterious, yet profoundly relevant to the believer's life today.

### The Language of the Spirit

Praying in tongues, also known as speaking in tongues, is the utterance of a language that is not comprehensible to the speaker's conscious mind. Instead, it is a language inspired and empowered by the Holy Spirit. This experience is often referred to as "glossolalia," derived from the Greek words "glossa" (tongue) and "laleo" (speak).

At its core, praying in tongues is a manifestation of the Holy Spirit's presence and power in the life of a believer. It is a direct and intimate form of communication with God that transcends the limitations of human language. In the Book of Acts, we find the inaugural account of this phenomenon on the Day of Pentecost, when the disciples were filled with the Holy Spirit and began to speak in languages they had not learned, enabling them to communicate the Gospel to a diverse crowd.

A Mystical Connection

Praying in tongues serves as a mystical connection between the believer's spirit and the Holy Spirit. When one prays in tongues, it is often described as an overflow of the heart's deepest longings and emotions, expressed in a language that bypasses the intellect. It is a form of worship that transcends the boundaries of human understanding, allowing the individual to pour out their innermost thoughts and feelings directly to God.

Beyond Words

One of the most extraordinary aspects of praying in tongues is its ability to go beyond the limitations of human vocabulary. In conventional prayer, we may struggle to find the right words to express our emotions or convey the depths of our hearts to God. However, when we pray in tongues, the Holy Spirit takes over, articulating our needs, desires, and praises in a language that is perfect in its expression. It is as if the Holy Spirit becomes our divine translator, ensuring that our prayers align with God's will.

Building Spiritual Edifices

The Apostle Paul, in his first letter to the Corinthians, provides valuable insights into the purpose and significance of praying in tongues. He refers to it as speaking "mysteries" in the spirit (1 Corinthians 14:2). This implies that when we pray in tongues, we engage in a form of spiritual revelation and insight. It's as if we are co-laborers with the Holy Spirit in building a spiritual edifice, one brick of revelation at a time.

Imagine your life as a grand cathedral, each prayer in tongues adding a unique, intricately carved stone to its structure. These stones represent hidden wisdom, divine strategies, and heavenly perspectives that can only be unearthed through the language of the Spirit. As you pray in tongues, you are contributing to the construction of a spiritual masterpiece that extends into eternity.

Bypassing the Mind

Praying in tongues bypasses the limitations of the conscious mind. When we pray in our native language, our intellect is engaged, and our prayers can sometimes be hindered by doubt, distraction, or self-consciousness. However, when we pray in tongues, our intellect takes a back seat, allowing our spirit to connect directly with God. It's a form of prayer that transcends doubt and self-criticism, enabling us to pray with boldness and confidence.

A Weapon of Spiritual Warfare

Another remarkable dimension of praying in tongues is its role in spiritual warfare. In Ephesians 6:18, Paul encourages believers to pray in the Spirit on all occasions with all kinds of prayers and requests. This spiritual warfare involves battling not against flesh and blood but against spiritual forces of evil. Praying in tongues equips us with a potent weapon in this battle, as it allows the Holy Spirit to intercede on our behalf with perfect prayers, piercing through the darkness and dismantling the enemy's strongholds.

A Personal Encounter with the Divine

For many believers, praying in tongues is a deeply personal encounter with the divine. It's a sacred space where they can lay bare their souls, trusting that the Holy Spirit understands their deepest needs, fears, and hopes. It's a form of communion with God that transcends human language, fostering intimacy and trust in the relationship between the believer and their Creator.

Praying in tongues is a unique and powerful gift given to believers by the Holy Spirit. It's a practice that defies easy explanation but holds immense value in the life of a Christian. It is a bridge between the finite and the infinite, a direct line of communication with the Divine, and a weapon of spiritual warfare. Embrace this gift with an open heart, for in doing so, you open yourself to a deeper, more profound relationship with the Holy Spirit and a richer prayer life that defies the ordinary and embraces the extraordinary.

## Chapter 13

## Discerning the Voice of the Holy Spirit in Prayer

In the realm of Christian spirituality, discerning the voice of the Holy Spirit is a topic of paramount importance. It is not merely an esoteric concept but a tangible and profound experience that can revolutionize your prayer life. In this chapter, we will delve into the depths of discernment, exploring the intricacies of recognizing and interpreting the voice of the Holy Spirit during prayer. Prepare to embark on a journey that will sharpen your spiritual senses and lead you to a closer walk with God.

The Still, Small Voice

The Bible tells us in 1 Kings 19:12, "And after the earthquake, there was a fire, but the Lord was not in the fire; and after the fire, a still small voice." This verse vividly illustrates how the voice of the Holy Spirit often comes as a gentle whisper amidst the chaos of our lives. To discern this voice, we must cultivate an environment of stillness and attentiveness.

Practice Silence and Solitude

In a world filled with noise and distraction, the practice of silence and solitude is a spiritual discipline that cannot be underestimated. Find a quiet place where you can retreat from the cacophony of daily life. Silence your mind and heart, and patiently wait on the Holy Spirit. It is in this hushed sanctuary that the voice of God becomes clearer.

Tune Your Spiritual Ears

Just as a musician tunes their instrument, we must tune our spiritual ears to hear the Holy Spirit's voice. Spend time in the Word of God, for it is the primary medium through which God speaks. Meditate on Scripture, and as you do, you will find that passages come alive with new meaning as the Holy Spirit imparts understanding and insight.

Distinguishing the Holy Spirit's Voice

In the symphony of thoughts and emotions that fill our minds, how do we distinguish the Holy Spirit's voice from our own inner monologue or external influences? Here are some keys to discernment:

Consistency with Scripture

The Holy Spirit will never contradict the Word of God. His voice aligns with the principles, teachings, and character of Christ as revealed in the Bible. If you receive a message during prayer that contradicts Scripture, it is not from the Holy Spirit.

Peace and Conviction

The Holy Spirit often speaks with a sense of peace and conviction. His guidance brings a settled assurance and a deep knowing. When you hear His voice, there is an inner confirmation that transcends mere human understanding.

Confirming Signs

God occasionally confirms His guidance with signs or circumstances that align with His will. Be attentive to divine providence, recognizing that the Holy Spirit can orchestrate events to affirm His voice.

Developing Spiritual Discernment

Discernment is not an instant skill but a lifelong journey. It requires a heart hungry for God's presence and a willingness to submit to His guidance. Here are practical steps to develop your spiritual discernment:

Pray Continually

Maintaining an ongoing conversation with God throughout your day keeps your spiritual senses attuned to His presence. The more you seek Him, the more attuned you become to His voice.

Seek Wise Counsel

Proverbs 11:14 reminds us, "Where there is no guidance, a people falls, but in an abundance of counselors, there is safety." Seek the wisdom of mature believers who can provide insight and confirmation when you are unsure about a message you've received.

Test the Spirits

In 1 John 4:1, we are exhorted to "test the spirits to see whether they are from God." Be diligent in discerning the origin of the thoughts and impressions that come during prayer. The Holy Spirit's voice will withstand scrutiny and align with Scripture.

Embrace Patience

Spiritual discernment is a process that unfolds over time. Do not be discouraged if you do not immediately recognize the voice of the Holy Spirit. Be patient, persistent, and trust that God will reveal Himself to you as you seek Him.

The Transformative Power of Discernment

Discerning the voice of the Holy Spirit in prayer is not an academic exercise; it is a life-transforming encounter with the living God. When you truly hear His voice, it can lead to profound changes in your life. You may receive guidance, comfort, correction, or inspiration that propels you into God's perfect will for your life.

Discerning the voice of the Holy Spirit in prayer is a sacred and mysterious journey. It requires a heart surrendered to God, a commitment to seeking His presence, and a discerning spirit honed through the practice of listening in stillness. As you embark on this journey, remember the promise of Jesus in John 10:27, "My sheep hear my voice, and I know them, and they follow me." May you hear and follow the voice of the Good Shepherd as you deepen your prayer life and draw nearer to God.

**Chapter 14**

## The Holy Spirit's Role in Spiritual Warfare

In the realm of Christian spirituality, the concept of spiritual warfare conjures images of epic battles between good and evil, angels and demons, and the very essence of our faith being put to the test. This chapter explores the extraordinary and often misunderstood role of the Holy Spirit in the midst of this cosmic struggle. We delve into the depths of spiritual warfare with a laser focus on detailed information, shedding light on the intricacies of this supernatural battle from a Christian perspective.

The Battlefield of the Mind

Before we delve into the Holy Spirit's role in spiritual warfare, it's essential to grasp the nature of the battle. The battleground is not a physical one but a battlefield of the mind and spirit. The apostle Paul aptly described it in Ephesians 6:12: "For we do not wrestle against flesh and blood, but against the rulers, against the authorities, against the cosmic powers over this present darkness, against the spiritual forces of evil in the heavenly places."

The mind is the primary battlefield, where thoughts, emotions, and desires collide. It is here that the enemy seeks to sow doubt, fear, and confusion. The Holy Spirit, as our divine ally, enters this battlefield with a divine arsenal.

The Armor of God

Ephesians 6:13-18 introduces the concept of the "Armor of God." Each piece of this spiritual armor is a manifestation of the Holy Spirit's power:

1. The Belt of Truth: The Holy Spirit is the Spirit of Truth (John 16:13). He empowers us to discern falsehood and deception in the spiritual realm, ensuring we stand firmly rooted in God's truth.

2. The Breastplate of Righteousness: The Holy Spirit convicts us of sin and leads us to righteousness (John 16:8). His presence within us serves as a shield against the enemy's accusations.

3. The Shoes of the Gospel of Peace: The Holy Spirit equips us to carry the message of God's peace to a troubled world. He guides our steps in spreading the gospel.

4. The Shield of Faith: The Holy Spirit ignites and strengthens our faith. He bolsters our belief in God's promises, making our faith an impenetrable shield against the enemy's fiery darts.

5. The Helmet of Salvation: The Holy Spirit assures us of our salvation in Christ (Ephesians 1:13). This confidence in our eternal security safeguards our minds from doubt and despair.

6. The Sword of the Spirit: The Word of God is the sword of the Spirit, and the Spirit himself empowers us to wield it effectively. Through the Holy Spirit, Scripture becomes a potent weapon in our spiritual warfare.

7. Prayer in the Spirit: Perhaps the most powerful weapon in our arsenal is prayer, especially when led by the Holy Spirit. He intercedes for us with groanings too deep for words (Romans 8:26), aligning our prayers with God's will.

Demonic Strongholds

To understand the Holy Spirit's role in spiritual warfare, we must acknowledge the existence of demonic strongholds. These are areas of our lives or regions in the spiritual realm where the enemy has established a foothold. These strongholds can manifest as addiction, unforgiveness, generational curses, or even spiritual oppression.

The Holy Spirit is the divine demolisher of strongholds (2 Corinthians 10:4). His power and authority shatter the chains that bind us and tear down the fortresses the enemy has erected. When we invite the Holy Spirit to work in these areas of our lives, we witness miraculous transformation and freedom.

Discerning Spirits

Central to spiritual warfare is the gift of discerning spirits (1 Corinthians 12:10). The Holy Spirit imparts this gift to believers, allowing them to perceive the spiritual realm more clearly. Discernment helps us identify not only the schemes of the enemy but also the presence of angelic assistance.

It's essential to remember that the Holy Spirit empowers us to discern not only the evil but also the good. He reveals God's plans, strategies, and purposes, guiding us to align our actions with the divine will.

Strategic Prayer and Warfare

Prayer, when empowered by the Holy Spirit, becomes a strategic tool in spiritual warfare. The Holy Spirit often leads believers to engage in intercessory prayer, targeting specific spiritual battles and strongholds.

These prayers are not based on human wisdom but on divine insight received through the Spirit.

Additionally, the Holy Spirit may reveal the need for fasting and spiritual disciplines as part of the warfare strategy. Fasting, coupled with prayer, amplifies the believer's spiritual authority and focus, creating an atmosphere where the enemy's influence diminishes.

The Holy Spirit, our Supreme Ally

In the cosmic struggle of spiritual warfare, the Holy Spirit is not a mere bystander but the supreme ally. He equips, empowers, and guides believers in their battles against the forces of darkness. As we put on the full armor of God and engage in strategic prayer, we partner with the Holy Spirit to claim victory over the enemy's schemes.

The Holy Spirit's role in spiritual warfare is nothing short of extraordinary. He is the divine force that ensures our triumph in the ongoing battle for our minds, hearts, and souls. With the Holy Spirit as our prayer partner and guide, we can boldly face the spiritual challenges that confront us, knowing that in Christ, we are more than conquerors.

## Chapter 15

# Walking in the Spirit and Effective Prayer

In the realm of Christian faith, the concept of "walking in the Spirit" is often discussed but not always fully understood. It's a phrase that carries profound significance, as it directly relates to our ability to engage in effective and transformative prayer. In this chapter, we will embark on a journey into the depths of what it means to walk in the Spirit and how it enhances our prayer life.

The Divine Dance of the Trinity

To comprehend walking in the Spirit, we must first grasp the intricate dance of the Holy Trinity - Father, Son, and Holy Spirit. Imagine the eternal and harmonious ballet of love and communion between these divine persons. The Holy Spirit is not an afterthought but an essential part of this dance, orchestrating the movements of creation, redemption, and sanctification.

As believers, we are invited to join this divine dance, not as mere spectators but as active participants. Walking in the Spirit means stepping onto the dance floor of the Trinity, moving in rhythm with the Holy Spirit's lead. It's an intimate partnership that transforms our prayer life from a monologue into a captivating dialogue with the Almighty.

The Spirit as Our Prayer Partner

In the act of prayer, we often approach God with our own agenda and requests. While our petitions are valid, walking in the Spirit means allowing the Holy Spirit to take the lead. Think of the Holy Spirit as your divine prayer partner, someone who knows the mind of God intimately and can guide your prayers in alignment with His will.

When you yield to the Holy Spirit in prayer, you become attuned to His promptings. Your requests align with God's purposes, and your prayers become more effective. It's not about eloquent words or a lengthy laundry list of desires; it's about intimacy with the Spirit and a willingness to be led by Him.

Surrendering Control

Walking in the Spirit requires surrendering control. It's akin to a dance where one partner must trust the other's lead completely. In prayer, this means letting go of our preconceived notions, fears, and doubts. It means trusting that the Holy Spirit knows precisely what to pray for, even when we don't.

The Apostle Paul beautifully articulates this in Romans 8:26-27 (NIV): "In the same way, the Spirit helps us in our weakness. We do not know what we ought to pray for, but the Spirit himself intercedes for us through wordless groans. And he who searches our hearts knows the mind of the Spirit because the Spirit intercedes for God's people in accordance with the will of God."

Praying in Tongues

One extraordinary aspect of walking in the Spirit is the practice of praying in tongues, also known as glossolalia. This spiritual gift allows the Holy Spirit to pray through you, bypassing your limited understanding and articulation. It's a unique form of prayer that transcends human language.

Praying in tongues is not a frivolous or random act but a powerful mode of communication with God. It's like having a direct hotline to the throne room of heaven. When you pray in tongues, you surrender your intellect and allow the Spirit to intercede on your behalf with perfect alignment to God's will.

Living a Transformed Life

Walking in the Spirit extends beyond prayer; it's a lifestyle. When you walk in the Spirit, you're guided by love, joy, peace, patience, kindness, goodness, faithfulness, gentleness, and self-control—qualities known as the fruit of the Spirit (Galatians 5:22-23).

This transformed way of living not only enhances your prayer life but also impacts every facet of your existence. Your relationships, decisions, and reactions are influenced by the Spirit, making you a vessel of God's grace and an instrument of His will.

A Dynamic Prayer Life

Walking in the Spirit and effective prayer are intrinsically intertwined. When you engage in this divine dance, your prayers cease to be routine recitations and become a dynamic conversation with the Creator. Your heart aligns with His purposes, and your petitions carry the weight of heaven's authority.

To walk in the Spirit is to embark on an extraordinary journey of faith and intimacy with God. It's a bold and out-of-the-ordinary way of living that transforms not only your prayer life but your entire existence. Embrace the Holy Spirit as your prayer partner, surrender control, and let the divine dance of the Trinity elevate your prayers to new heights of effectiveness and intimacy.

## Chapter 16

## Praying for Others with the Holy Spirit's Help

In the tapestry of Christian faith, intercessory prayer is the golden thread that weaves together the body of believers. It is a divine calling, a sacred duty, and a profound privilege to lift up the needs and concerns of others before the throne of grace. But how do we engage in this ministry of intercession with the utmost effectiveness and divine empowerment? The answer lies in partnering with the Holy Spirit.

### The Power of Intercessory Prayer

Before we delve into the role of the Holy Spirit in intercessory prayer, let's first grasp the immense significance of this spiritual discipline. Intercessory prayer is a dynamic act of love and selflessness. It bridges the gap between human need and God's abundant grace. It is an act of obedience to Christ's command to love our neighbors as ourselves (Matthew 22:39) and to bear one another's burdens (Galatians 6:2).

Intercession has the power to transform lives, heal brokenness, and bring about miraculous interventions. When we pray for others, we step into the gap between their struggles and God's provision. It's like becoming a spiritual bridge that connects the earthly with the heavenly. It's a divine partnership where we become co-laborers with God in His redemptive work.

### The Holy Spirit: Our Prayer Partner

Now, let's shift our focus to the Holy Spirit's vital role in intercessory prayer. The Holy Spirit is not just a passive observer of our prayers; He is an active participant, a divine prayer partner who empowers us in this ministry.

1. Spiritual Discernment: One of the Holy Spirit's primary functions in intercession is to provide us with spiritual discernment. He enables us to perceive the hidden needs, struggles, and burdens of those we are praying for. Through the Holy Spirit, we can pray specifically and effectively, addressing the root issues rather than just the surface symptoms.

2. Praying in Tongues: In 1 Corinthians 14:2, we are told that when we pray in tongues, we speak mysteries in the spirit. This means that the Holy Spirit, through the gift of tongues, allows us to intercede on behalf of others with a divine language that transcends our human understanding. It's like having a direct line to heaven, where the Spirit prays through us with perfect alignment to God's will.

3. Boldness and Persistence: The Holy Spirit infuses us with boldness and persistence in our intercession. He empowers us to approach God's throne with confidence (Hebrews 4:16), knowing that our prayers are aligned with His divine purpose. When we partner with the Spirit, we can boldly ask for God's intervention in the lives of others, believing that He is a faithful and loving Father.

4. Spiritual Warfare: Intercession often involves spiritual warfare, as we contend for the souls and destinies of those we pray for. The Holy Spirit equips us with spiritual weapons and strategies to wage effective warfare against the forces of darkness. He guides us in praying against spiritual strongholds and breaking chains of bondage.

An Extraordinary Example: George Müller

To illustrate the profound impact of intercessory prayer empowered by the Holy Spirit, let's look at the life of George Müller. Müller was a 19th-century Christian who cared for thousands of orphans in England. He never made his needs known publicly but relied solely on prayer. Müller and his fellow believers would gather for prayer, and astonishingly, every need was met without fail. This man of faith prayed specifically and persistently, believing in God's faithfulness. The Holy Spirit guided him and those who prayed with him, leading to remarkable answers to prayer.

Practical Steps for Praying with the Holy Spirit's Help

1. Surrender to the Spirit: Begin by surrendering yourself to the Holy Spirit. Invite Him to lead and guide your intercession. Acknowledge your dependence on Him for insight, wisdom, and empowerment.

2. Listen and Discern: Spend time in silence, listening to the Holy Spirit. Allow Him to reveal the specific needs and concerns of those you are interceding for. The Spirit may bring to mind people or situations that require your prayerful attention.

3. Pray in Tongues: If you have the gift of tongues, don't hesitate to use it in your intercession. Trust that the Holy Spirit is interceding through you with perfect prayers aligned with God's will.

4. Persist in Prayer: Intercessory prayer is often a marathon, not a sprint. Be persistent and don't give up. The Holy Spirit will sustain your passion and burden for those you are praying for.

5. Declare God's Promises: Incorporate Scripture into your intercession. Declare God's promises over the lives of those you are praying for. The Word of God is powerful and effective (Isaiah 55:11).

6. Pray with Thanksgiving: As you intercede, don't forget to thank God for His faithfulness and for the privilege of partnering with Him in prayer.

A Divine Partnership

Intercessory prayer is a divine partnership between believers and the Holy Spirit. It is an extraordinary act of love and obedience that has the power to transform lives and nations. When we yield to the Holy Spirit, He equips us with discernment, boldness, and persistence in our intercession. Through Him, we can pray with divine precision and expect miraculous answers.

As you continue on your journey of intercessory prayer, remember that you are not alone. The Holy Spirit is your prayer partner, empowering you to impact the world through the fervent and effective prayers you offer on behalf of others. Embrace this partnership, and watch as God's redemptive work unfolds through your intercession.

## Chapter 17

# The Holy Spirit and the Gift of Wisdom in Prayer

In the journey of faith, we often find ourselves at the crossroads of life's decisions, facing dilemmas that require not just our knowledge, but divine wisdom. It is in these pivotal moments that the Holy Spirit shines as the source of supernatural wisdom in our prayers. In this chapter, we will delve deeply into the profound connection between the Holy Spirit and the gift of wisdom in prayer, exploring how it can guide us in making life-altering decisions.

The Nature of Wisdom

Wisdom is a prized virtue in the Christian faith, often mentioned in the Bible as a quality to be sought after earnestly. Proverbs 2:6 tells us, "For the LORD gives wisdom; from his mouth come knowledge and understanding." Yet, how does this wisdom differ from worldly knowledge? It is not merely the accumulation of facts and information but a divine insight that enables us to see beyond the surface of things.

When we pray for wisdom, we are essentially seeking the ability to perceive God's will and apply it to our lives. This wisdom transcends human reasoning and taps into a deeper, spiritual realm. It aligns our desires with God's purposes, making our prayers a powerful force for His kingdom.

The Holy Spirit as the Source of Wisdom

To understand the connection between the Holy Spirit and the gift of wisdom, we must first recognize the Holy Spirit's role in the Godhead. In Christian theology, the Holy Spirit is the third person of the Trinity, co-equal and co-eternal with the Father and the Son. He is the paraclete, the comforter, and the guide promised by Jesus in John 16:13: "But when he, the Spirit of truth, comes, he will guide you into all the truth."

This guidance into truth includes the wisdom we seek in our prayers. The Holy Spirit, being intimately connected to the Father and the Son, possesses divine wisdom and imparts it to believers. When we invite the Holy Spirit into our prayers, we open the door to receive this supernatural wisdom.

Praying for Wisdom

Praying for wisdom is not a casual request; it is an acknowledgment of our dependence on God's guidance in all aspects of life. James 1:5 encourages us, saying, "If any of you lacks wisdom, you should ask God, who gives generously to all without finding fault, and it will be given to you."

When we pray for wisdom, we are essentially inviting the Holy Spirit to work in our hearts and minds. This prayer is an act of surrender, an admission that we don't have all the answers but trust God to lead us. It aligns our desires with His divine purpose.

The Intersection of Wisdom and Discernment

Wisdom in prayer often intersects with discernment. Discernment is the ability to distinguish between good and evil, to recognize the leading of the Holy Spirit amidst the noise of the world. In 1 Corinthians 2:14, we read, "The person without the Spirit does not accept the things that come from the Spirit of God but considers them foolishness."

In the act of praying for wisdom, we invite discernment as well. The Holy Spirit grants us the discernment to recognize God's voice amidst the many competing voices in our lives. This discernment becomes particularly crucial when we face complex decisions, moral dilemmas, or times of confusion.

The Wisdom of Solomon

One of the most famous examples of divine wisdom in the Bible is the story of Solomon. In 1 Kings 3:9-12, Solomon asked for wisdom when God offered to grant him anything he desired. God not only gave him wisdom but also bestowed upon him riches and honor beyond measure.

Solomon's wisdom was not born of human intellect but was a gift from God through the Holy Spirit. It enabled him to judge wisely, resolve disputes, and lead his people with justice. His story reminds us that when we seek divine wisdom through prayer, God can bless us in ways we cannot fathom.

How the Holy Spirit Imparts Wisdom

The process of receiving wisdom from the Holy Spirit is not always immediate or apparent. It often involves a journey of spiritual growth and maturity. Here are some ways the Holy Spirit imparts wisdom in our lives:

1. Through Scripture:
The Bible is a wellspring of divine wisdom. The Holy Spirit illuminates its pages, revealing hidden truths and guiding us in applying its principles to our lives.

2. Through Prayer and Meditation:

As we spend time in prayer and meditation, the Holy Spirit speaks to our hearts, offering insights and understanding that transcend human reasoning.

3. Through Counsel and Guidance:
The Holy Spirit can use trusted mentors and fellow believers to provide guidance and counsel in our decisions. He often confirms His wisdom through the voices of others.

4. Through Inner Peace:
God's wisdom is often accompanied by a sense of peace. When we are uncertain about a decision, the Holy Spirit can grant us a deep inner peace as a confirmation of His guidance.

5. Through Experience:
Over time, as we walk in obedience to God's leading, we gain experiential wisdom. The Holy Spirit helps us learn from our successes and failures, shaping us into wiser individuals.

The Courage to Follow Divine Wisdom

Praying for wisdom is not a mere intellectual exercise. It requires the courage to follow the guidance we receive, even when it contradicts our human understanding or desires. This courage comes from a deep trust in God's sovereignty and love for us.

The story of Mary, the mother of Jesus, is a beautiful illustration of this courage. When the angel Gabriel appeared to her with the news that she would conceive a child by the Holy Spirit, Mary didn't fully grasp the implications, but she responded with faith and submission, saying, "I am the Lord's servant. May your word to me be fulfilled." (Luke 1:38).

Mary's example teaches us that divine wisdom often leads us on unexpected paths, but if we have the courage to follow, God's purposes are fulfilled in remarkable ways.

## The Transformative Power of Wisdom

Divine wisdom, imparted by the Holy Spirit, has the power to transform our lives and impact the world around us. It equips us to make decisions that align with God's will and to navigate the complexities of our journey with grace and insight.

When we operate in this wisdom, our prayers become more than petitions; they become instruments of God's divine purpose. We see answers to our prayers that go beyond our expectations because we are praying in alignment with His wisdom.

## A Life Guided by Divine Wisdom

In this chapter, we have explored the profound connection between the Holy Spirit and the gift of wisdom in prayer. Divine wisdom, rooted in the wisdom of God Himself, is not a mere intellectual pursuit but a transformational force in the lives of believers.

As you continue your journey of faith, remember that the Holy Spirit is your constant companion, ready to impart divine wisdom in your prayers. Embrace the courage to follow His guidance, trust in His sovereignty, and watch as your life unfolds according to His divine plan. In the partnership of prayer with the Holy Spirit, you will discover a wisdom that surpasses all understanding, leading you into a life of purpose and fulfillment in Christ.

## Chapter 18

## Cultivating a Heart of Gratitude in Prayer

In the journey of faith, gratitude is like the radiant sun that dispels the clouds of doubt and despair. It's a spiritual attitude that not only enriches our connection with the divine but also transforms the way we perceive and interact with the world around us. In this chapter, we will delve into the profound importance of cultivating a heart of gratitude in your prayer life from a Christian perspective. Prepare to embark on a spiritual exploration that will help you develop an unshakable attitude of thankfulness.

The Foundation of Christian Gratitude

At the core of Christian gratitude lies the acknowledgment of God as the ultimate source of all blessings. It's the realization that every good and perfect gift comes from Him (James 1:17). When you begin your prayers with gratitude, you're acknowledging God's sovereignty and His boundless love for you.

But Christian gratitude isn't just about thanking God for the blessings you've received; it's about recognizing the beauty of His character. It's about understanding that even in the midst of trials and tribulations, God is still worthy of praise because of who He is.

The Power of Gratitude in Prayer

Gratitude isn't merely a polite way to say "thank you" to God; it's a transformative force that can revolutionize your prayer life. Let's explore some of the profound ways in which cultivating a heart of gratitude can impact your relationship with God and your journey of faith:

1. Gratitude Shifts Your Perspective:

When you start your prayers by thanking God for His blessings, you shift your focus away from your problems and toward His provision. Instead of dwelling on what you lack, you celebrate what you have, which leads to a more positive outlook on life.

2. Gratitude Deepens Your Trust:

Trust and gratitude are intimately connected. When you express thankfulness for what God has done in the past, you're essentially saying, "I trust You for the future." This deepens your faith and reliance on God's divine guidance.

3. Gratitude Fuels Joy:

A heart overflowing with gratitude is a heart filled with joy. It's impossible to be genuinely thankful and remain in a state of despair or bitterness. Gratitude not only brightens your own spirit but also blesses those around you.

4. Gratitude Opens the Door to Intimacy:

Gratitude is the key that unlocks the door to intimacy with God. When you're thankful for His presence in your life, you become more aware of His nearness. This awareness fosters a deeper, more intimate connection with the divine.

Cultivating a Heart of Gratitude

Now that we've explored the significance of gratitude in prayer, let's delve into practical ways to cultivate this attitude in your daily life:

1. Keep a Gratitude Journal:

Start a journal where you daily record things you're thankful for. This simple practice helps you become more aware of God's blessings, no matter how small they may seem.

2. Practice Mindfulness:

Pay attention to the present moment and intentionally seek out reasons to be thankful. In the beauty of a sunrise, the laughter of a child, or the warmth of a friend's embrace, you'll find opportunities to express gratitude.

3. Thank God in All Circumstances:

Challenge yourself to thank God in both good times and bad. Even in the midst of trials, you can find reasons to be grateful, such as the opportunity for growth and the promise of His unwavering presence.

4. Share Your Gratitude:

Don't keep your gratitude to yourself. Share it with others through acts of kindness, encouraging words, and a willingness to lend a helping hand. Your gratitude can inspire gratitude in others.

5. Cultivate an Attitude of Humility:

Recognize that everything you have is a gift from God. This understanding fosters humility, which in turn deepens your gratitude.

In the grand tapestry of your Christian faith, gratitude is a vibrant thread that weaves its way through every aspect of your spiritual journey. It's an attitude that not only enriches your prayer life but also transforms your entire perspective on life. By cultivating a heart of gratitude, you'll discover a deeper, more intimate relationship with God and a profound sense of joy that transcends circumstances.

As you close this chapter, take a moment to reflect on the blessings in your life, both big and small. Offer a prayer of gratitude to the Creator who loves you unconditionally and has bestowed upon you the gift of His presence. Embrace the transformative power of gratitude, and let it illuminate your path on this remarkable journey of faith.

## Chapter 19

## Hearing God's Voice through the Holy Spirit

In the journey of faith, one of the most profound and intimate experiences a Christian can have is hearing God's voice through the Holy Spirit. It's a moment when the divine transcends the human, and the Creator speaks directly to the created. This chapter delves deep into this extraordinary phenomenon, exploring the nuances, challenges, and blessings of discerning God's voice through the Holy Spirit.

The Whisper of the Divine

Imagine standing on the edge of a vast, still lake on a calm morning. The waters are so tranquil that you can see your own reflection. In much the same way, hearing God's voice through the Holy Spirit often begins as a gentle whisper. It's that soft, subtle prompting in your heart that nudges you toward a certain decision, a particular path, or a specific action. Like the ripple that starts small but eventually spreads across the entire lake, this whisper can lead to a profound transformation of your life.

The Symphony of Silence

In a world filled with noise, finding the sacred silence where God's voice can be heard is a challenge. Yet, it is in these moments of quiet contemplation, meditation, and prayer that the Holy Spirit often chooses to speak most clearly. Picture a magnificent symphony hall, where every note of a divine masterpiece is composed in the stillness between the sounds. Similarly, God's voice emerges in the pauses and silences between our own thoughts and words.

The Language of Love

God's voice through the Holy Spirit is a language of love. It speaks to our deepest needs, desires, and fears. It comforts us in times of sorrow and guides us in moments of uncertainty. It's a language that transcends words, a communication of the heart. It's not just about hearing words; it's about feeling the presence of the Divine in your soul. It's like a warm embrace that assures you of God's unfailing love and guidance.

The Art of Discernment

Discerning God's voice from the cacophony of our own thoughts and external influences requires practice and patience. It's like learning to differentiate between the various instruments in an orchestra. You need to train your spiritual ears to recognize the unique timbre of God's voice. This discernment often comes through spending time in the Scriptures, seeking wise counsel, and developing a deep, personal relationship with the Holy Spirit.

Embracing the Unexpected

God's voice through the Holy Spirit doesn't always come in the ways we expect. It can be a sudden insight during your morning coffee, a dream that lingers in your mind, or a feeling of conviction that won't let go. It's like stumbling upon a hidden treasure when you least expect it. Be open to the unexpected, for God's voice can manifest in the most surprising and unconventional ways.

The Challenge of Surrender

Hearing God's voice through the Holy Spirit often requires surrendering our own will and desires. It's about aligning our hearts with God's divine plan, even when it contradicts our own ambitions. Surrender is like handing the conductor's baton to God and letting Him lead the symphony of your life. It's a surrender that brings harmony and purpose to our existence.

The Fear Factor

Fear can be a significant obstacle to hearing God's voice. We fear making the wrong decision, misinterpreting His guidance, or even facing the reality of what He might ask of us. Yet, remember that God's perfect love casts out fear. Trust in His goodness and His promise to guide you, and fear will lose its grip.

Experiencing the Miraculous

When you truly hear God's voice through the Holy Spirit, it can lead to miraculous outcomes. It's like witnessing a breathtaking display of fireworks in the night sky. Your obedience to His voice can result in transformed lives, answered prayers, and a deeper connection with the divine. These moments remind us that God's plans are far greater than our own.

The Eloquent Whisper

Hearing God's voice through the Holy Spirit is a journey of faith, a divine conversation that requires tuning our hearts to the frequency of heaven. It's a language of love, a symphony of silence, and an art of discernment. It challenges us to surrender, overcome fear, and embrace the unexpected. In the end, it is the eloquent whisper of the Divine that leads us on a path of purpose, fulfillment, and everlasting joy.

## Chapter 20

## Praying for Healing with the Holy Spirit's Anointing

In the realm of faith, there exists an extraordinary power—the power of healing through the Holy Spirit's anointing. This chapter delves into the depths of this divine phenomenon, exploring the intricate and sacred connection between prayer, healing, and the anointing of the Holy Spirit from a Christian perspective.

The Healing Power of the Holy Spirit

To understand the Holy Spirit's role in healing, we must first grasp the concept of divine healing itself. In the Christian faith, healing goes beyond mere physical restoration; it encompasses the mending of body, mind, and spirit. It is the profound intervention of God's grace into our lives, bringing wholeness in every dimension.

The Anointing: A Divine Transfer

Anointing, in the biblical context, signifies a divine transfer of God's power and presence. It is a consecration, setting apart, and empowering for a specific purpose. In the Old Testament, we see prophets, priests, and kings anointed with oil as a symbol of God's favor and equipping for their respective roles.

In the New Testament, the concept of anointing takes on a new dimension through the person of Jesus Christ. He is referred to as the "Anointed One" or the Messiah. It is through Jesus that the anointing flows to believers. This anointing is the presence of the Holy Spirit dwelling within us, empowering us to do the works of Jesus, including healing the sick.

The Role of Faith

Faith serves as the conduit through which the Holy Spirit's healing power flows. It is not blind faith but a confident assurance in God's willingness and ability to heal. Jesus often emphasized the importance of faith in the healing process, saying, "Your faith has made you well" (Mark 5:34).

The Prayer of Faith

Central to the Christian perspective on healing is the prayer of faith, which James 5:14-15 highlights:

"Is anyone among you sick? Let them call the elders of the church to pray over them and anoint them with oil in the name of the Lord. And the prayer offered in faith will make the sick person well; the Lord will raise them up. If they have sinned, they will be forgiven."

This passage illuminates the connection between anointing, prayer, and healing. The anointing with oil symbolizes the presence of the Holy Spirit, while the prayer of faith activates His healing power.

The Laying on of Hands

In the New Testament, we often see Jesus and the apostles laying hands on the sick when praying for their healing. This physical touch serves as a point of contact for the transfer of God's healing power through the Holy Spirit. It is an act of faith that amplifies the connection between the anointing and the person in need.

Practical Steps for Praying for Healing with the Holy Spirit's Anointing

1. Surrender to the Holy Spirit: Begin by acknowledging your dependence on the Holy Spirit. Surrender your desires and agenda to His guidance.

2. Pray in Faith: Approach God with unwavering faith in His ability and willingness to heal. Believe that the anointing of the Holy Spirit is present and active.

3. Anoint with Oil: While anointing with oil is symbolic, it serves as a tangible reminder of the Holy Spirit's presence. Use it as an act of consecration.

4. Lay Hands: If possible, lay hands on the person in need of healing. This physical touch reinforces the connection between the anointing and the recipient.

5. Speak the Word: Declare healing Scriptures and promises over the person. God's Word is powerful and aligns your prayers with His will.

6. Listen to the Holy Spirit: Be attentive to any promptings or impressions from the Holy Spirit during the prayer. He may guide you in specific actions or words of knowledge.

7. Persevere in Prayer: Healing may not always manifest instantly. Continue to pray in faith, trusting in God's timing and wisdom.

Testimonies of Healing

Throughout Christian history, countless testimonies bear witness to the miraculous healings that have occurred through the Holy Spirit's anointing. These stories serve as reminders that the power of healing is not confined to the past but is accessible to believers today.

Praying for healing with the Holy Spirit's anointing is a sacred journey of faith, a journey that transcends the ordinary and taps into the extraordinary power of God. It is a demonstration of God's love and compassion for His children, an affirmation of His presence in our lives, and a testament to the profound connection between prayer, faith, and the anointing of the Holy Spirit. As you embark on this journey, may your faith soar, your prayers be fervent, and the healing touch of the Holy Spirit be a reality in the lives of those you pray for.

## Chapter 21

## The Holy Spirit and Praying for God's Will

In the realm of Christian faith, one of the most profound and transformative aspects of prayer is seeking and praying for God's will. It's a concept that's often discussed, yet its true depth and significance are sometimes overlooked. In this chapter, we will delve into the heart of this matter, exploring how the Holy Spirit plays a pivotal role in aligning our prayers with God's divine purpose.

The Challenge of Aligning with God's Will

Praying for God's will can be challenging, especially in a world filled with distractions and our own desires. As humans, we often have our own agendas, ambitions, and dreams, which can cloud our ability to discern and accept God's will for our lives. It's a paradoxical struggle - our desire for control versus our longing to surrender to the Creator's greater plan.

Yet, this is where the Holy Spirit steps in as our divine guide. The Holy Spirit serves as a bridge between our limited human perspective and God's infinite wisdom. It is through the Spirit's guidance that we can begin to pray in alignment with God's will.

The Role of the Holy Spirit in Discernment

Discerning God's will is not a mere intellectual exercise; it is a spiritual journey that requires humility, patience, and a willingness to listen. The

Holy Spirit equips us with the tools needed for this endeavor. It is the Spirit who opens our spiritual eyes and ears, helping us perceive God's leading in our lives.

Imagine a scenario where you stand at a crossroads, unsure of which path to take. It's in these moments that the Holy Spirit acts as a divine GPS, guiding us in the direction that aligns with God's perfect plan. Through prayer, meditation, and silence, we can attune our hearts to the gentle whisper of the Spirit, which leads us to God's will.

Submission and Surrender

Praying for God's will requires a profound sense of submission and surrender. It involves acknowledging that God's thoughts are higher than our thoughts, and His ways are beyond our comprehension. The Holy Spirit empowers us to let go of our own desires and trust in God's goodness.

This surrender is not a passive resignation but an active choice to trust in God's sovereignty. The Holy Spirit empowers us with the faith needed to say, "Not my will, but Yours be done." It's a declaration of ultimate trust in the Creator's wisdom and love.

Transformation Through Prayer

As we align our prayers with God's will, something remarkable happens – we are transformed. Our desires begin to align with His desires, our purposes with His purposes. The Holy Spirit works within us to mold us into vessels of God's grace and instruments of His divine plan.

This transformation is not only inward but also outward. Our actions, decisions, and interactions with others reflect the love and wisdom of

God. We become conduits of His grace, carrying out His will in the world.

## The Power of Persistent Prayer

Persistence in prayer is another dimension where the Holy Spirit plays a significant role. In the process of seeking God's will, there may be moments of confusion or doubt. However, the Holy Spirit empowers us to persevere in prayer, even when the path seems unclear.

We are reminded of the parable of the persistent widow in Luke 18. She kept going to the unjust judge until he granted her justice. How much more will our loving Father answer our prayers when we persistently seek His will? The Holy Spirit sustains our faith and resolve during these seasons of waiting.

## A Life of Adventure

Praying for God's will isn't a mundane or passive endeavor. It's an invitation to a life of adventure, purpose, and fulfillment. When we surrender to God's will and allow the Holy Spirit to guide our prayers, we step into a divine narrative that transcends our human limitations.

In the Bible, we see individuals like Abraham, Moses, David, and Mary, who embraced God's will and experienced extraordinary journeys. Their lives were marked by faith, obedience, and a willingness to say "yes" to God's calling. The Holy Spirit empowers us to walk a similar path, filled with divine surprises and meaningful impact.

## The Partnership of a Lifetime

Praying for God's will with the laser focus of the Holy Spirit is a partnership of a lifetime. It's an ongoing dialogue where we submit our desires, align our hearts with God's, and trust in His wisdom. It's an adventure where we discover God's purpose for our lives and participate in His redemptive plan for the world.

As we continue our journey in faith, may we be ever attuned to the Holy Spirit's guidance, and may our prayers resound with the beautiful harmony of God's will. Through this partnership, we not only find our truest selves but also become agents of transformation in a world hungering for the divine.

## Chapter 22

# The Holy Spirit's Comfort in Times of Sorrow

In the depths of sorrow, when our hearts ache and tears seem to be our only solace, the Holy Spirit emerges as a profound source of comfort and solace for Christians. This chapter explores the extraordinary and often overlooked role of the Holy Spirit in times of sorrow, shedding light on how the Spirit's presence can transform our grief into a profound encounter with God's love and grace.

The Divine Comforter

Christianity teaches us about the Holy Trinity: God the Father, God the Son (Jesus Christ), and God the Holy Spirit. In times of sorrow, it is the Holy Spirit who reveals Himself as the Divine Comforter. The Bible assures us in 2 Corinthians 1:3-4: "Praise be to the God and Father of our Lord Jesus Christ, the Father of compassion and the God of all comfort, who comforts us in all our troubles so that we can comfort those in any trouble with the comfort we ourselves receive from God."

This verse beautifully illustrates that the comfort we receive from the Holy Spirit is not merely for our own benefit but equips us to become instruments of comfort to others as well. It's a divine exchange, where the Spirit's consolation in our sorrow empowers us to bring solace to others in their times of need.

The Empathy of the Spirit

One of the most profound aspects of the Holy Spirit's role in times of sorrow is His ability to empathize with our pain. Unlike well-meaning friends or family members who may offer words of comfort but can't fully understand our grief, the Holy Spirit enters into our suffering with perfect empathy. Romans 8:26 tells us that the Spirit intercedes for us "with groans that words cannot express." In our deepest moments of sorrow, when we can't find the right words to pray, the Spirit intercedes on our behalf, articulating our pain to God.

Imagine the comfort of knowing that the Creator of the universe, through the Holy Spirit, not only hears our cries but feels our anguish with an empathy beyond human comprehension. In our moments of despair, we are never alone.

Transforming Sorrow into Worship

Sorrow has a way of clouding our vision, making it difficult to see beyond the pain. However, the Holy Spirit can transform our sorrow into an opportunity for worship and spiritual growth. In the midst of grief, we are often forced to confront our own limitations, vulnerabilities, and dependence on God. It is in this vulnerability that the Spirit's work is most profound.

Consider the story of Job in the Old Testament. Job endured unimaginable suffering, yet he proclaimed, "The Lord gave, and the Lord has taken away; blessed be the name of the Lord" (Job 1:21). Job's ability to worship in the midst of sorrow was not born out of sheer willpower but was a result of the Holy Spirit's presence in his life. The Spirit empowers us to transcend our circumstances and find comfort in the unchanging nature of God.

A Deeper Relationship with God

Sorrow can be a catalyst for deepening our relationship with God through the Holy Spirit. In our moments of brokenness, we are often more receptive to the Spirit's guidance and presence. It is in these times that we discover the intimacy of our relationship with God is not dependent on our emotional state but on the unwavering faithfulness of the Spirit.

The Apostle Paul, who faced numerous trials and tribulations, wrote about the transformative power of the Holy Spirit in 2 Corinthians 12:9-10: "But he said to me, 'My grace is sufficient for you, for my power is made perfect in weakness.' Therefore, I will boast all the more gladly about my weaknesses so that Christ's power may rest on me. That is why, for Christ's sake, I delight in weaknesses, in insults, in hardships, in persecutions, in difficulties. For when I am weak, then I am strong."

Paul recognized that it was in his weakness and times of sorrow that the Holy Spirit's power was most evident. In our moments of vulnerability, we have the opportunity to experience the strengthening and transformative work of the Spirit.

Embracing the Comfort of the Holy Spirit

In times of sorrow, the Holy Spirit is not an abstract theological concept but a tangible and compassionate presence. The Spirit empathizes with our pain, transforms our grief into worship, deepens our relationship with God, and equips us to comfort others. As Christians, we can take solace in knowing that even in our darkest moments, the Comforter is with us, guiding us toward the light of God's love and grace. Embrace the Holy Spirit's comfort, for it is a divine gift that transcends the boundaries of human understanding, offering hope and healing in the midst of sorrow.

## Chapter 23

## Praying with the Fruit of Patience and the Holy Spirit

In the journey of faith and prayer, few virtues are as challenging and rewarding as patience. Patience is often described as a "fruit of the Spirit" in Christian theology, and when coupled with the guidance of the Holy Spirit, it becomes a potent force in our prayer lives. In this chapter, we will delve into the profound connection between patience, the Holy Spirit, and the transformative power they wield in our conversations with the Divine.

The Nature of Patience

Before we explore the partnership of patience and the Holy Spirit in prayer, let's first grasp the essence of patience. In the hustle and bustle of our modern lives, patience is a virtue that often seems in short supply. It is the ability to endure delays, difficulties, and adversity without becoming anxious or frustrated. It's not merely about waiting but about waiting well. In the realm of prayer, patience takes on a unique dimension.

Patience in Prayer

In the realm of prayer, patience takes on a unique dimension. It's about waiting expectantly, trusting that God's timing is perfect. We live in an era of instant gratification, where we expect answers to our prayers as soon as we utter them. However, God operates on His own timetable, which may not align with our immediate desires.

Patience in prayer involves surrendering our own sense of urgency and trusting that God knows what is best for us. It's an acknowledgment that His wisdom surpasses our understanding, and His plans are far greater than our own. As the Apostle Paul reminds us in Romans 8:25 (NIV), "But if we hope for what we do not yet have, we wait for it patiently."

The Holy Spirit as our Guide

Now, let's introduce the Holy Spirit into this equation. The Holy Spirit is often referred to as our Comforter, Counselor, and Guide. When we invite the Holy Spirit into our prayer life, we are essentially opening the door to divine wisdom and discernment. The Spirit intercedes for us with groanings too deep for words, aligning our prayers with God's will (Romans 8:26-27).

When we pray with the fruit of patience, we allow the Holy Spirit to guide us through the waiting period. The Spirit helps us to remain calm, trust in God's plan, and continue seeking His face even when our prayers seem unanswered. It's like having a divine GPS navigating us through the twists and turns of life, ensuring we stay on the path of faith.

The Power of Persistent Prayer

Patience and persistence in prayer go hand in hand. Jesus himself encouraged us to be persistent in our petitions to God. In Luke 18:1-8, He told the parable of the persistent widow who kept coming to an unjust judge seeking justice. The judge, out of annoyance, eventually granted her request. Jesus used this parable to illustrate that if even an unjust judge could be moved by persistence, how much more will our loving Father respond to our persistent prayers.

When we pray with patience and persistence, we align ourselves with the heart of God. We demonstrate our faith that He is in control and that His timing is perfect. We acknowledge that our requests may not be fulfilled immediately, but we trust that they will be answered in the way that is best for us.

The Transformation of Character

Praying with the fruit of patience and the Holy Spirit's guidance is not just about getting what we want when we want it. It's about transforming our character. As we wait patiently and persistently, we grow in faith, hope, and love.

Patience cultivates humility as we recognize our limited understanding and control. It fosters empathy as we learn to wait alongside others who are also in need. It deepens our dependence on God and strengthens our relationship with Him.

In the grand tapestry of prayer, patience, and the Holy Spirit are threads that intricately weave together. When we embrace patience as a fruit of the Spirit and invite the Holy Spirit into our prayer lives, we are embarking on a transformative journey. We learn to wait with hope, trust in God's wisdom, and persistently seek His will.

As you continue to develop your prayer life, remember that patience is not a passive waiting but an active trust in God's faithfulness. Allow the Holy Spirit to be your guide, leading you through the waiting periods and helping you grow in faith and character. In this partnership, you will find that the answers to your prayers, though they may not always come on your schedule, are always perfectly timed according to God's divine plan.

## Chapter 24

## The Holy Spirit's Role in Strengthening Your Faith

In the journey of faith, there comes a time when doubt creeps in, when the storms of life shake the very foundation of your beliefs. It's during these trying moments that the Holy Spirit steps forward as the divine catalyst of unwavering faith, like the calm within the storm. This chapter will delve into the extraordinary ways the Holy Spirit strengthens your faith, from igniting the spark of belief to sustaining it through life's most challenging trials.

The Spark of Belief

Faith, in its essence, is a spark—a tiny, radiant ember that can set your heart ablaze with the divine truth of God's existence and love. The Holy Spirit's first role in strengthening your faith is to ignite this spark. Imagine a dark room with a single candle; that's the state of your heart before the Holy Spirit's touch. When the Holy Spirit enters your life, it's as though a gust of wind sweeps through, causing the flame to dance and grow brighter.

The Holy Spirit awakens your spiritual senses, allowing you to perceive the divine in the ordinary. Suddenly, you notice God's fingerprints in the beauty of creation, in the kindness of a stranger, and in the words of Scripture. Your belief in God's presence and love becomes tangible, and that tiny spark of faith transforms into a burning passion.

The Gift of Discernment

Faith isn't blind; it's discerning. The Holy Spirit equips you with the gift of discernment, an extraordinary ability to recognize the voice of God amidst the noise of the world. This divine discernment becomes your compass, guiding you through life's complex decisions and moral dilemmas.

Through the Holy Spirit, you develop an uncanny sense of right and wrong, an inner voice that whispers truth when deception lurks nearby. The Holy Spirit empowers you to decipher God's will in your life, to see His purpose in every circumstance, and to trust His plan even when it seems counterintuitive.

Empowering Prayer

Prayer is the lifeline of faith, and the Holy Spirit empowers your prayers in extraordinary ways. It's not just a monologue but a dialogue with the divine. When you pray, the Holy Spirit intercedes on your behalf, translating your deepest groans and desires into words that resonate with God's heart.

This divine partnership in prayer transcends the mundane and enters the realm of the miraculous. It's where the impossible becomes possible, where healing and deliverance occur, and where you witness the power of faith in action. The Holy Spirit teaches you to pray with boldness, persistence, and faith that moves mountains.

Comfort in Trials

Life is riddled with trials and tribulations, and it's during these moments that your faith is tested most severely. Yet, the Holy Spirit provides extraordinary comfort. He's the gentle presence that whispers, "I am with you," when you're overwhelmed by grief or fear.

The Holy Spirit doesn't just offer empty words of solace; He brings tangible peace that surpasses understanding. He weaves a tapestry of hope in the midst of despair, reminding you that even in the darkest valleys, God is still in control. It's through these trials that your faith is forged like pure gold, refined by the fire of adversity.

Empowerment for Kingdom Impact

Faith isn't a solitary endeavor; it's a call to make an impact in the world. The Holy Spirit empowers you with extraordinary gifts and talents to serve God's kingdom. These gifts are not for self-glorification but for the advancement of God's purposes on Earth.

Under the Holy Spirit's guidance, your faith becomes a force for change—a catalyst for healing, justice, and love. You become an instrument of God's grace, touching lives in ways you never imagined. Your faith takes on a mission, a purpose beyond personal salvation, and you become part of God's grand narrative of redemption.

An Extraordinary Faith

The Holy Spirit's role in strengthening your faith is nothing short of extraordinary. He takes the ember of belief and fans it into a blazing fire. He equips you with discernment, empowers your prayers, comforts you in trials, and empowers you for kingdom impact. Your faith, when nurtured by the Holy Spirit, becomes a vibrant, dynamic force that not only sustains you but transforms the world around you.

As you journey in faith, never underestimate the power of the Holy Spirit within you. He is the extraordinary force that makes your faith unshakeable, unbreakable, and unparalleled. Embrace His presence, trust His guidance, and let your faith shine brightly in a world in desperate need of the extraordinary hope only faith in Christ can bring.

# Chapter 25

# Praying for Guidance and Direction with the Holy Spirit

In the journey of faith, there are moments when we stand at crossroads, faced with decisions that could potentially shape the course of our lives. In these pivotal moments, we often find ourselves seeking divine guidance and direction. We long for a clear path, a sign, or a word from above to illuminate the way forward. In this chapter, we will delve deep into the profound relationship between prayer, the Holy Spirit, and the pursuit of divine guidance.

The Holy Spirit: Our Divine GPS

Imagine the Holy Spirit as your divine GPS, constantly guiding you through the twists and turns of life's intricate roadways. Just as a GPS device relies on a satellite connection to provide real-time directions, our connection to the Holy Spirit is our lifeline to the divine navigation system. This connection is forged through prayer, and it is in prayer that we tap into the infinite wisdom of God.

Prayer as a Two-Way Conversation

Prayer is often viewed as a monologue, where we present our requests and petitions to God. However, it is essential to recognize that prayer is a dialogue, not a one-sided conversation. It's not just about us talking to God; it's about God speaking to us through the Holy Spirit. When we pray for guidance, we open the door for divine communication.

Listening to the Whisper of the Spirit

In the hustle and bustle of life, the voice of the Holy Spirit can be a gentle whisper amidst the cacophony. To hear this whisper clearly, we must cultivate an environment of stillness and receptivity in our hearts and minds. This requires intentional silence, meditation, and a willingness to patiently wait upon the Lord.

The Bible tells us in 1 Kings 19:12 that God's voice came to Elijah not in the powerful wind, earthquake, or fire but in a "gentle whisper." Similarly, the Holy Spirit often speaks softly, and we must attune our spiritual ears to catch His divine counsel.

Discerning the Promptings of the Spirit

Once we've created an atmosphere for hearing the Holy Spirit's guidance, the next step is discernment. The Holy Spirit may speak through a variety of means: through Scripture, through a sudden conviction in our hearts, through the counsel of wise mentors, or even through circumstances aligning in a particular way. Discernment involves testing what we sense against the character of God, His Word, and His purposes.

The Peace that Passes Understanding

One profound way the Holy Spirit guides us is through the inner peace He provides. When we pray for guidance and direction, the Spirit often imparts a sense of peace about a particular course of action. Philippians 4:7 speaks of "the peace of God, which surpasses all understanding." This peace is like a compass, pointing us in the right direction and affirming God's will.

The Role of Scripture in Guidance

God's Word, the Bible, is a treasure trove of wisdom and guidance. The Holy Spirit illuminates the Scriptures, making them a lamp to our feet and a light to our path (Psalm 119:105). When seeking direction, immerse yourself in the Word, and allow the Spirit to reveal its relevance to your situation. Sometimes, a verse you've read many times before can suddenly come alive with newfound significance.

Praying for Confirmation

In critical decisions, it is wise to seek confirmation through prayer. This involves presenting your request multiple times to God and asking for affirmation. Gideon, in the Old Testament, sought confirmation from God twice (Judges 6:36-40). The Holy Spirit can confirm His guidance through dreams, visions, or a persistent sense of conviction in your heart.

Trusting in God's Sovereignty

Finally, as we seek guidance and direction, we must remember that God's ways are higher than our ways (Isaiah 55:8-9). Sometimes, the guidance we receive may not align with our preconceived notions or desires. Trusting in God's sovereignty means surrendering our will to His and acknowledging that His plan is ultimately for our good (Romans 8:28).

When we pray for guidance and direction with the Holy Spirit as our guide, we step into a realm where the divine intersects with the earthly. It is a journey of faith, trust, and listening. Through prayer, discernment, and an open heart, we can confidently navigate life's complex choices, knowing that the Holy Spirit is our unwavering companion on this remarkable journey of faith.

## Chapter 26

## The Holy Spirit's Role in Answered Prayer

In the realm of Christian faith, prayer holds a sacred place. It's the bridge between the finite and the infinite, the earthly and the divine. We often pray with hope, faith, and expectation, seeking answers to our petitions. But have you ever considered the dynamic role of the Holy Spirit in the process of answered prayer? In this chapter, we will delve deeply into this extraordinary partnership between believers and the Holy Spirit, exploring the nuanced ways in which the Spirit actively participates in bringing about answered prayers.

The Divine Interpreter

Imagine prayer as a conversation between you and the Creator of the universe. You may utter your requests, desires, and hopes, but sometimes words alone fall short. The Holy Spirit acts as the divine interpreter, translating the groanings of your heart into a language understood by God. As the Apostle Paul wrote in Romans 8:26-27:

"Likewise the Spirit helps us in our weakness. For we do not know what to pray for as we ought, but the Spirit himself intercedes for us with groanings too deep for words. And he who searches hearts knows what is the mind of the Spirit, because the Spirit intercedes for the saints according to the will of God."

Here, we see the Holy Spirit bridging the gap, taking our imperfect petitions and aligning them with God's perfect will. Your heartfelt sighs, unspoken longings, and even your tears are understood by the Holy Spirit and conveyed to the Father in a language beyond words.

Spiritual Discernment

The Holy Spirit provides an invaluable gift: discernment. In the process of prayer, this gift becomes a guiding light, helping us distinguish between our own desires and God's will. Often, our prayers are clouded by our limited understanding, selfish ambitions, and worldly perspectives. But the Spirit sheds light on the path of righteousness, enabling us to pray in alignment with God's purposes.

To illustrate this, consider the story of Jesus in the Garden of Gethsemane. In Matthew 26:39, He prayed, "My Father, if it be possible, let this cup pass from me; nevertheless, not as I will, but as you will." Here, we witness Jesus' humanity wrestling with the divine plan. Yet, in His moment of vulnerability, the Holy Spirit empowered Him to submit to the Father's will. The Spirit provided the discernment to recognize that God's purpose was greater than His immediate desire.

Praying in Tongues

An aspect of prayer often misunderstood but profoundly significant is the gift of speaking in tongues, also known as glossolalia. This gift, imparted by the Holy Spirit, allows believers to pray in a heavenly language. While the Apostle Paul acknowledges that speaking in tongues may be a mystery to the one who prays (1 Corinthians 14:2), it plays a unique role in connecting us with the divine.

Speaking in tongues transcends the limitations of human language, providing a direct channel for the Spirit's communication with God. In 1 Corinthians 14:14-15, Paul affirms the importance of this spiritual gift: "For if I pray in a tongue, my spirit prays, but my mind is unfruitful.

What am I to do? I will pray with my spirit, but I will pray with my mind also; I will sing praise with my spirit, but I will sing with my mind also." Here, we see that praying in tongues engages the depths of our spirit, allowing the Holy Spirit to articulate prayers that are in perfect harmony with God's will.

Empowering Boldness

The Holy Spirit empowers believers with boldness in their prayers. When faced with adversity, opposition, or uncertainty, the Spirit infuses us with the courage to approach the throne of grace with confidence. In Hebrews 4:16, we are encouraged: "Let us then with confidence draw near to the throne of grace, that we may receive mercy and find grace to help in time of need."

This boldness is not arrogance; rather, it is the assurance that comes from knowing we are indwelt by the Spirit of God. We can approach God with our requests, knowing that the Spirit is our advocate and helper in prayer. This confidence enables us to pray audaciously, believing that God is both able and willing to answer according to His wisdom and purpose.

Co-Laborers with the Spirit

In the grand tapestry of God's plan, believers are not passive recipients of answered prayers. Instead, we are co-laborers with the Holy Spirit. 1 Corinthians 3:9 reminds us, "For we are God's fellow workers. You are God's field, God's building." Our prayers are not detached from God's divine agenda but are intricately woven into His sovereign plan.

The Holy Spirit invites us into partnership, prompting us to align our prayers with God's heart. When we pray, we are not merely making requests; we are participating in the unfolding of God's purposes on earth. This partnership amplifies the impact of our prayers, making them more than words but powerful instruments of transformation.

The Holy Spirit's role in answered prayer is profound and multifaceted. As believers, we are privileged to have the Holy Spirit as our divine interpreter, our guide in discernment, our enablement in speaking in tongues, our source of boldness, and our co-laborer in God's kingdom work.

Understanding and embracing the Holy Spirit's role in prayer enriches our spiritual journey and deepens our relationship with the Creator. It moves us from mere petitioners to co-participants in the divine unfolding of God's will on earth. As you continue your prayer journey, remember the active presence and partnership of the Holy Spirit, for in this divine collaboration, prayers become more than words—they become channels of God's transformative power.

# Chapter 27

# Partnering with the Holy Spirit for Spiritual Growth

In the journey of faith, one of the most exhilarating and transformative experiences a Christian can encounter is partnering with the Holy Spirit for spiritual growth. It's a journey that transcends the ordinary, for it is in this partnership that believers find themselves propelled into the extraordinary realm of divine transformation, deep intimacy with God, and supernatural empowerment.

The Holy Spirit as the Catalyst for Growth

To embark on this extraordinary journey, it's vital to understand the Holy Spirit's role as the catalyst for spiritual growth. The Holy Spirit is not a distant, abstract concept but a dynamic, personal presence of God dwelling within every believer. In John 14:16-17, Jesus promises the Holy Spirit to His disciples: "And I will ask the Father, and he will give you another Helper, to be with you forever, even the Spirit of truth, whom the world cannot receive because it neither sees him nor knows him. You know him, for he dwells with you and will be in you."

This indwelling Spirit, the Holy Spirit, is the divine force that ignites the flames of transformation within our hearts and souls. He is the One who guides us, empowers us, and continually leads us into all truth (John 16:13). Recognizing the Holy Spirit as a divine Person, not just an abstract force, is crucial for our spiritual growth.

Surrendering to the Spirit's Leading

Partnering with the Holy Spirit begins with a radical surrender of our wills to His guidance. It's not about trying harder or achieving more through human effort but rather about yielding to the divine wisdom and power that reside within us.

Imagine a sailboat on a calm sea. No matter how much effort the sailors put into rowing or navigating, the boat won't move without the wind. Similarly, our efforts to grow spiritually can be in vain if we don't rely on the wind of the Holy Spirit. Surrendering control of our lives to the Spirit is like hoisting the sail and allowing Him to guide us toward the destination of spiritual maturity.

The Role of Spiritual Disciplines

Partnering with the Holy Spirit isn't passive; it involves active participation on our part. Spiritual disciplines such as prayer, Bible study, fasting, worship, and meditation are the means through which we cooperate with the Spirit's work.

Prayer: Prayer is the channel through which we commune with God and hear His voice. When we pray in the Spirit, we align our desires with God's will, allowing Him to shape our hearts and minds.

Bible Study: The Word of God is the lamp to our feet and the light to our path (Psalm 119:105). By regularly immersing ourselves in Scripture, we open ourselves to the Holy Spirit's teaching, correction, and transformation.

Fasting: Fasting is a powerful discipline that helps us crucify the desires of the flesh and tune in to the Spirit's leading. It's a way of saying, "Not my will, but Yours be done."

Worship: Worship is more than singing songs; it's a lifestyle of surrender and adoration. In worship, we invite the presence of the Holy Spirit to fill us, transforming us from the inside out.

Meditation: Meditating on God's Word and His goodness allows us to renew our minds (Romans 12:2). It's a practice that deepens our understanding of His ways and aligns our thoughts with His.

The Fruit of the Spirit

As we partner with the Holy Spirit, we begin to bear the fruit of the Spirit mentioned in Galatians 5:22-23: love, joy, peace, patience, kindness, goodness, faithfulness, gentleness, and self-control. These are not mere attributes to cultivate but manifestations of the Spirit's presence within us.

Consider the fruit of love. In partnering with the Holy Spirit, our capacity to love expands beyond the limits of human affection. We find ourselves loving even the unlovable, forgiving the unforgivable, and demonstrating a supernatural love that reflects the very nature of God.

Empowerment for Kingdom Impact

Partnering with the Holy Spirit doesn't stop at personal transformation; it extends to the empowerment for kingdom impact. Acts 1:8 declares, "But you will receive power when the Holy Spirit has come upon you, and you will be my witnesses in Jerusalem and in all Judea and Samaria, and to the end of the earth."

This power is not for personal glory but for the advancement of God's kingdom. It empowers us to share the Gospel boldly, heal the sick, cast out demons, and demonstrate God's love in practical ways. It's a divine partnership that equips us to be agents of change in a broken world.

Embracing the Supernatural

To fully partner with the Holy Spirit for spiritual growth, we must embrace the supernatural. The Spirit operates in the realm of the supernatural, and as we yield to His leading, we step into a reality where miracles, signs, and wonders become a natural part of our Christian walk.

Imagine praying for the sick and witnessing their miraculous healing. Envision speaking words of wisdom and knowledge by the Spirit's revelation. Picture yourself being used by God to impact lives in ways that defy human explanation. This is the realm of the supernatural that becomes accessible through partnership with the Holy Spirit.

Partnering with the Holy Spirit for spiritual growth is an adventure of a lifetime. It's a journey that takes us beyond the ordinary into the extraordinary, where the mundane becomes sacred, and the impossible becomes possible. As we surrender, engage in spiritual disciplines, bear the fruit of the Spirit, and embrace the supernatural, we become vessels through which God's glory shines brightly in a world that desperately needs His light. So, take the leap of faith, partner with the Holy Spirit, and watch your spiritual growth soar to new heights, for with the Spirit as your guide, there are no limits to what you can become in Christ.

## Chapter 28

## Praying for Revival with the Holy Spirit's Fire

In a world filled with distractions, chaos, and moral decline, the call for revival within the Christian community has never been more urgent. Revival is not a mere religious event; it is a spiritual awakening that ignites the hearts of believers and transforms communities, bringing them back to the fervent faith of their ancestors. This chapter will delve into the profound and transformative concept of praying for revival with the Holy Spirit's fire.

The Biblical Foundation of Revival

Before we embark on our journey to understand how to pray for revival, let us lay a solid biblical foundation. Throughout the Old and New Testaments, we find numerous instances of revival, where God's people experienced a renewal of faith and a return to righteousness. The essence of revival is deeply rooted in God's desire for His people to live in communion with Him, to be holy as He is holy.

One of the most striking examples of revival is found in 2 Chronicles 7:14, where God speaks to King Solomon: "If my people, who are called by my name, will humble themselves and pray and seek my face and turn from their wicked ways, then I will hear from heaven, and I will forgive their sin and will heal their land." This verse highlights the prerequisites for revival: humility, prayer, seeking God's face, and repentance from sin. It is not a passive event; it requires active engagement with God.

The Holy Spirit's Role in Revival

The Holy Spirit is the catalyst for revival. He is often referred to as the "fire" that ignites the hearts of believers and purifies their lives. In the book of Acts, we witness the outpouring of the Holy Spirit on the day of Pentecost, a momentous event that marked the birth of the early Church. Tongues of fire rested on the disciples, empowering them to boldly proclaim the gospel. This fire of the Holy Spirit is the same fire that we seek when praying for revival.

The Holy Spirit's role in revival can be understood through several key aspects:

1. Conviction of Sin: The Holy Spirit convicts individuals of their need for salvation. In times of revival, this conviction intensifies, leading to genuine repentance and turning away from sin.

2. Spiritual Passion: The Holy Spirit ignites a passionate love for God and His Word. Believers hunger and thirst for righteousness, desiring a deeper relationship with their Creator.

3. Spiritual Gifts: Revival often brings an outpouring of spiritual gifts. The Holy Spirit equips believers with gifts such as prophecy, healing, and tongues to edify the body of Christ and reach the lost.

4. Unity and Fellowship: The Holy Spirit unifies believers, breaking down divisions and fostering a sense of community. In revival, Christians come together in love and harmony, emphasizing the importance of the Church as the body of Christ.

Praying for Revival: The Holy Spirit's Fire

Now, let us delve into the heart of this chapter: how to pray for revival with the Holy Spirit's fire. It is not a formulaic process but a passionate pursuit of God's presence. Here are some principles to guide your prayers:

1. Seek God's Face: Begin by seeking God's face in prayer. Spend time in His presence, worshiping Him for who He is. Ask the Holy Spirit to reveal any areas of your life that need repentance and surrender.

2. Intercede for Others: Revival is not limited to individual transformation but extends to entire communities and nations. Intercede fervently for your church, your community, and your nation, asking the Holy Spirit to move mightily.

3. Pray for Hunger and Thirst: Pray for a hunger and thirst for righteousness to consume your heart and the hearts of others. Ask the Holy Spirit to ignite a passionate desire to know God more deeply.

4. Expect the Supernatural: Trust in the Holy Spirit's power to bring about supernatural manifestations in the midst of revival. Be open to the gifts of the Spirit and the miraculous.

5. Repent and Surrender: Continually repent and surrender to the work of the Holy Spirit in your life. Let go of anything that hinders your intimacy with God.

6. Stay Persistent: Revival may not happen overnight. Continue to pray with perseverance, believing that God hears your prayers and will respond in His perfect timing.

The Impact of Revival

When revival comes with the Holy Spirit's fire, its impact is far-reaching and transformative:

1. Spiritual Awakening: Believers experience a renewed zeal for God, resulting in personal transformation and a renewed commitment to holiness.

2. Salvations: Many individuals who were far from God come to faith in Christ through the powerful witness of believers and the conviction of the Holy Spirit.

3. Social Transformation: Communities affected by revival often see a decrease in crime, an increase in acts of kindness, and a general moral upturn.

4. Global Impact: Revival can have a global impact as well, as missionaries are raised up and sent out to share the gospel with unreached people groups.

Praying for revival with the Holy Spirit's fire is not a mere religious exercise but a passionate pursuit of God's presence and transformation. It involves seeking God's face, interceding for others, and surrendering to the work of the Holy Spirit. When revival comes, it brings about spiritual awakening, salvation, and a profound impact on society. As Christians, let us continue to fervently pray for revival, believing in the power of the Holy Spirit to bring about a mighty move of God in our lives and in the world.

## Chapter 29

# The Holy Spirit's Presence in Times of Worship and Prayer

In the journey of faith, there are moments when words fail, and the depths of the heart seek communion with the Divine. These are the moments when worship and prayer converge, and it is in these sacred spaces that the Holy Spirit's presence is most profoundly felt. In this chapter, we will delve into the extraordinary connection between the Holy Spirit, worship, and prayer, exploring how these elements interweave to create an experience that transcends the ordinary and ushers believers into the supernatural realm.

The Sanctified Dance of Worship

Worship is more than a series of songs or hymns; it is a sacred dance of the soul. When we lift our voices in praise, we invite the Holy Spirit to join our celebration. It's not merely about melodies and harmonies but about the condition of our hearts. As we worship in spirit and in truth, the Holy Spirit hovers, ready to fill the atmosphere with His presence.

Picture a worship service where voices rise in unity, hands are raised in surrender, and tears flow in reverence. In those moments, the Holy Spirit descends like a gentle dove, bringing with Him an overwhelming sense of peace and joy. It is as if the boundaries of time and space fade away, and we stand on the precipice of eternity.

The Symphony of Tongues

In the midst of worship, the Holy Spirit often stirs believers to speak in tongues. This supernatural language is a direct connection to heaven, a language known only to God and His Spirit. It is a language of mysteries, a bridge between the earthly and the divine.

When the gift of tongues is exercised in the context of worship, it's as if a symphony of heavenly voices joins the earthly choir. It's an audacious act of faith, a declaration that we are not alone in our worship. The Holy Spirit takes the utterances of our hearts and translates them into a language that resonates in the courts of heaven.

Intercession Beyond Words

Prayer is the language of intimacy with God, and when coupled with worship, it becomes a powerful force that can shape the course of history. The Holy Spirit, our divine Prayer Partner, intercedes on our behalf when our words fall short. In those moments of worshipful prayer, the Spirit groans with us, understanding the deepest longings of our hearts.

Imagine a prayer meeting where believers gather not just to petition God but to worship Him in the process. As they sing songs of adoration, their prayers take on new dimensions. The Holy Spirit, who knows the mind of God, guides their intercessions, aligning them with the divine will.

The Manifestations of His Presence

When the Holy Spirit's presence is tangibly felt in times of worship and prayer, it often leads to manifestations of His power. Some may be overcome with a holy laughter, others may weep uncontrollably under the weight of His glory. Healings and miracles become commonplace as faith soars on the wings of worship.

In these moments, the ordinary boundaries of human experience are shattered. Believers may find themselves caught up in visions and dreams, receiving divine revelations and insights. It is as if the spiritual realm becomes more real than the physical, and heaven touches earth in ways that defy explanation.

Worship and Prayer as a Gateway

In the realm of faith, worship and prayer are not mere rituals; they are gateways to encountering the Holy Spirit in profound ways. They are the means by which we transcend the limits of the natural world and step into the supernatural. In these moments, the ordinary becomes extraordinary, the mundane becomes sacred, and our connection with God becomes palpable.

As we conclude this chapter, remember that the Holy Spirit's presence in times of worship and prayer is not reserved for a select few but is available to all who seek Him with sincerity and hunger. So, dare to step out of the ordinary, embrace the extraordinary, and let the Holy Spirit usher you into a realm of worship and prayer that defies explanation. In His presence, you will find that the boundaries between heaven and earth blur, and you become part of a divine symphony that echoes throughout eternity.

## Chapter 30

## Walking in Prayerful Partnership with the Holy Spirit

In this final chapter, we embark on a journey that encapsulates the culmination of our exploration into the profound relationship between the believer and the Holy Spirit. As we delve deeper into the concept of "Walking in Prayerful Partnership with the Holy Spirit," we will uncover the intricacies of this divine connection from a Christian perspective, reaching beyond the ordinary into the extraordinary.

The Divine Dance of Prayer

Imagine prayer as a sacred dance, where you are not the only dancer on the floor. The Holy Spirit is your eternal dance partner, guiding your every move with grace and precision. As you twirl through the steps of your daily life, the Holy Spirit leads, and you follow. This partnership extends to your prayer life, where you are no longer a solo performer but part of a divine duet.

Surrendering to the Lead

In the dance of prayerful partnership, surrender is key. Just as a dancer must trust their partner's lead, so must you trust the Holy Spirit's guidance. Surrendering means relinquishing your agenda and allowing the Holy Spirit to take the lead in your prayers. It's an act of humility, acknowledging that God's wisdom surpasses your own.

Listening to the Rhythm of Silence

One of the most profound aspects of walking in prayerful partnership is learning to listen to the rhythm of silence. In the busyness of life, we often fill our prayers with words, requests, and petitions. However, the Holy Spirit invites us to embrace moments of silence, where His presence speaks volumes. It's in the stillness that we can hear His gentle whispers and feel the nudges of His guidance.

Praying in the Spirit

To truly walk in prayerful partnership with the Holy Spirit, we must explore the depths of praying in the Spirit. This goes beyond our natural language and taps into the supernatural. When we pray in tongues, we allow the Holy Spirit to intercede on our behalf, aligning our prayers with the perfect will of God. It's a mysterious and beautiful form of communication between our spirit and the Spirit of God.

Divine Dreams and Visions

The Holy Spirit doesn't limit His communication to words alone. He often speaks through dreams and visions. These divine encounters can provide profound insights into God's plans and purposes for our lives. Learning to discern and interpret these dreams and visions is a vital aspect of walking in prayerful partnership.

Experiencing Miraculous Answers

When you walk in prayerful partnership with the Holy Spirit, be prepared for extraordinary answers to your prayers. Miracles become a part of your journey as you align your requests with God's heart. The Holy Spirit orchestrates divine interventions that leave you in awe of His power and love.

Acts of Compassion and Service

Walking in prayerful partnership with the Holy Spirit extends beyond your personal life. It leads to acts of compassion and service that touch the lives of others. The Holy Spirit empowers you to be a vessel of His love, bringing healing, hope, and transformation to those around you.

Walking in the Spirit Daily

Lastly, walking in prayerful partnership is not a one-time event but a daily lifestyle. It's about being in constant communion with the Holy Spirit, seeking His guidance in every decision, and allowing Him to transform you into the image of Christ. It's a journey of growth, sanctification, and intimacy with God.

In conclusion, "Walking in Prayerful Partnership with the Holy Spirit" is an extraordinary adventure that takes you beyond the ordinary realms of prayer. It's a divine dance where you surrender, listen, and participate in the miraculous. As you walk hand in hand with the Holy Spirit, your life becomes a testament to the boundless love and power of God. So, embrace this partnership with boldness and anticipation, for it will lead you to places and experiences that exceed your wildest expectations.

## Appreciation

Thank you for purchasing and reading my book. I am extremely grateful and hope you found value in reading it. Please consider sharing it with friends and family and leaving a review online.

Your feedback and support are always appreciated and allow me to continue doing what I love.

Please go to www.amazon.com
if you'd like to leave a review.

# TIMOTHY ATUNNISE's BESTSELLERS

**Deliverance & Spiritual Warfare**
- Monitoring spirits exposed and defeated
- Jezebel spirit exposed and defeated
- Marine spirits exposed and defeated
- Serpentine spirit exposed and defeated
- Prophetic warfare: Unleashing supernatural power in warfare
- Rise above the curse: An empowering guide to overcome witchcraft attacks
- The time is now: A guide to overcoming marital delay
- Earth moving prayers: Pray until miracles happen
- I must win this battle: Expanded edition
- I must my financial battle
- Essential prayers
- Open heavens: Unlocking divine blessings and breakthroughs
- This battle ends now
- Breaking the unbreakable
- Reversing evil handwriting
- I must win this battle - French edition
- I must win this battle - Spanish edition
- Ammunition for spiritual warfare
- Reversing the Irreversible
- Let there be a change
- Total Deliverance: Volume 1
- 21 days prayer for total breakthroughs
- Warrior Mom: Defending your children in the court of heaven.
- Breaking Chains of Rejection: A personal deliverance manual
- Overcoming afflictions in the workplace
- The art of spiritual vision casting
- Thriving beyond letdowns: Overcoming constant disappointments

- Breaking the Family Curse: Unraveling the Past for a Brighter Future and Transform Your Family Legacy
- The Anointed Intercessor: A Prayer Warrior's Calling
- Prayers of the Midnight Warriors
- Spiritual Mapping 101: A Beginner's Guide
- Deliverance from Satanic Dreams and Nightmares
- Inherited battles, victorious lives: Power to conquer ancestral strongholds and liberate your family's destiny

**Weapons of Warfare**
- The Name of Jesus: The unstoppable weapon of warfare
- Praise and Worship: Potent weapons of warfare
- Blood of Jesus: The ultimate weapon
- The Word of God as a weapon: A double-edged sword to bring transformation and unparallel victory in spiritual warfare.
- Praying with Power: The warrior's guide to weapon of dynamic warfare prayer
- The weapon of prophetic dreams
- Praying in tongues of heaven
- Waging war through fasting: The incontestable weapon of spiritual warfare
- The fire of God's presence: A weapon of unparallel strength & potency
- The Word of Testimony – A stealth weapon of spiritual warfare
- Angelic assistance in spiritual warfare
- The art of spiritual discernment: Your warfare advantage

**Power of Anointing**
- The power of anointing for success: Partnering with God in extraordinary moments for great success
- The Power of Anointing for Generational Wealth

**Holy Spirit**
- Holy Spirit my prayer partner

**14 Days Prayer & Fasting Series**
- 14 Days prayer to break evil patterns.
- 14 days prayer against delay and stagnation
- 14 days prayer for a new beginning
- 14 days prayer for deliverance from demonic attacks
- 14 days prayer for total healing
- 14 days prayer for deliverance from rejection and hatred
- 14 days prayer for healing the foundations
- 14 days prayer for breaking curses and evil covenants
- 14 days prayer for uncommon miracles
- 14 days prayer for restoration and total recovery
- 14 days prayer: It's time for a change
- 14 days prayer for deliverance from witchcraft attacks
- 14 days prayer for accelerated promotion
- 14 days prayer for deliverance from generational problems
- 14 days prayer for supernatural supply
- 14 days prayer to God's will for your life
- 14 days prayer for Mountaintop Experience
- 14 days prayer for home, family and marriage restoration
- 14 days prayer to overcome stubborn situations.
- 14 days prayer for restoration of stolen destiny
- 14 days prayer for financial breakthroughs

**Personal Finances**
- The art of utility bills negotiation
- From strapped to successful: Unlocking financial freedom beyond Paycheck to paycheck
- Escape the rat race: How to retire in five years or less.

- Mastering mean reversion: A guide to profitable trading, so simple a 10-year-old can understand

## Bible Study
- The King is coming
- Seven judgments of the Bible
- The miracle of Jesus Christ
- The book of Exodus
- Lost and found: The house of Israel
- The parables of Jesus Christ

## Fiction
- The merchant's legacy: A tale of faith and family
- A world unraptured: Brink of oblivion
- Gone: A chronicle of chaos

## Family Counseling
- Healing whispers: Biblical comfort and healing for men after miscarriage

## Leadership/Business
- The most intelligent woman: A woman's guide to outsmarting any room at any level
- Thriving in the unknown: Preparing children for careers that don't exist yet.
- Communication breakthrough: Cultivating deep connections through active listening
- Overcoming Procrastination
- Raising Christian Leaders: A Parent's Guide

## Spiritual Growth

- Divine Intimacy: Embracing the Transformative Power of Intimate Communion to Discover Profound Connection and Fulfillment
- 7 Steps to Receiving a Miracle
- 7 Simple Secrets to Consistent Answered Prayers

**Theology/Ministry**
- Laughing Pulpit: Using humor to enhance preaching.

**Parenting/Relationship**
- Embracing metamorphosis: Nurturing teenage girls' remarkable journey into adulthood

**Marriage/Family**
- The conscious husband: Mastering active listening in marriage.
- The conscious wife: Nurturing relationship with awareness, building a perfect and flourishing family.
- Conscious parenting: Mastering active listening to your children.
- From cradle to consciousness: Guiding your child's awareness
- The 'Not Tonight' syndrome: Overcoming false excuses in marital intimacy.

**End-Times**
- Dawn of eternity: Unraveling the rapture of the saints
- Signs of the end-times: Deciphering prophecies in a race against time
- The rise of the Antichrist: Unveiling the beast and the prophecies

Printed in Great Britain
by Amazon